Reforming the Christian Faith

Reforming the Christian Faith

Theological Interpretation after the Protestant Reformation

MARK W. KARLBERG

WIPF & STOCK · Eugene, Oregon

REFORMING THE CHRISTIAN FAITH
Theological Interpretation after the Protestant Reformation

Copyright © 2017 Mark W. Karlberg. All rights reserved. Except for brief quotations in critical publications or reviews, no part of this book may be reproduced in any manner without prior written permission from the publisher. Write: Permissions, Wipf and Stock Publishers, 199 W. 8th Ave., Suite 3, Eugene, OR 97401.

Wipf & Stock
An Imprint of Wipf and Stock Publishers
199 W. 8th Ave., Suite 3
Eugene, OR 97401

www.wipfandstock.com

PAPERBACK ISBN: 978-1-5326-3766-7
HARDCOVER ISBN: 978-1-5326-3767-4
EBOOK ISBN: 978-1-5326-3768-1

Manufactured in the U.S.A. SEPTEMBER 25, 2017

Permission to republish two articles in this volume as chapters five and six (with slight revision) has been granted by the Trinity Foundation (*The Trinity Review*)

Acknowledging with gratitude
And thanksgiving to God

The Van Til-Kline legacy

Extraordinary contributions
Bequeathed to Reformed theology

Soli Deo Gloria

Table of Contents

Preface | ix

Section One: The Development of Doctrine in the History of the Church

    Chapter One   The History of Doctrine: A Broad Overview | 3

    Chapter Two   Theological First-Principles: The Why and How of Thinking Biblically | 21

Section Two: The Formal and Material Principles of the Protestant Reformation

    Chapter Three   Revelation and Scripture: God's Covenantal Engagement | 39

    Chapter Four   God and Humanity: Eden Lost and Regained | 51

Section Three: Departure from Historic Reformed Federalism

    Chapter Five   Controversy within Present-Day Reformed Orthodoxy: Westminster Seminary in Philadelphia | 69

    Chapter Six   A Denomination Stakes Its Position: The Orthodox Presbyterian Church's Study on Republication | 87

    Chapter Seven   The Protestant Reformation Derailed: Closing a Chapter in the Still-Ongoing Theological Dispute | 113

Epilogue: Christ, Church, and Covenant: Christian Calling in the Reformed Tradition | 129

Bibliography | 137

Names Index | 143

Preface

THIS PUBLICATION MARKS THE 500th anniversary of the Protestant Reformation (October 31, 2017), a cause for both celebration and lament; celebration for the faithfulness of God in preserving the truth of the Gospel in many places of the Christian world, and lament for its decline in other places (some unexpectedly). The title of this collection of essays intends to convey two important aspects of Christian faith: (1) the expression of faith is in constant change over the course of history, for good or for ill; (2) the faith of the church is ever in need of reform (and correction) according to the teaching of Scripture. Of course, the slogan for the Reformed tradition is "reformed and always being reformed according to the Word of God" (*ecclesia reformata, semper reformanda*). The term "faith" itself comprehends both doctrine and life (the practice of biblical faith and ethics in the life of the individual believer and in the church corporately). In my estimate, Reformed theology offers the most consistent, biblically-based expression of the Christian faith. We owe a great debt to all those who labored to restate faithfully the teachings of Scripture, and who stood against teaching deemed contrary to Scripture. Oftentimes doctrine is forged in the midst of intense theological controversy.

The enduring legacy of Cornelius Van Til and Meredith G. Kline at Westminster Seminary is one of the great blessings in the history of Reformed Christianity. Regrettably, both theologians have been widely underappreciated and misinterpreted (in the latter instance due to conflicting teaching concerning the doctrine of the covenants). The Westminster tradition as borne by the two seminaries, one in Philadelphia and the other in Escondido, has been greatly mired in controversy in recent decades. Some efforts of reform have taken place in order to address heterodox teaching that has made its way

Preface

into the theological school (and the churches it serves). Defection from the two formative principles of the Reformation, the formal and material principles, has had an untold impact on the well-being of the seminary and the church. To be sure, it is not enough to affirm the full authority of Scripture: The problem has been its *rightful interpretation* (namely, acknowledgement and implementation of the principle that Scripture is self-interpreting, a critical feature of the principle of *sola Scriptura*). For those familiar with my writings, it comes as no surprise to hear me say again that the chief engine in the undoing of the Protestant Reformation in contemporary Reformed (federal) theology is the theological meanderings that have occurred in recent decades at Westminster Seminary in Philadelphia.

When serving on the faculty of Westminster Seminary, John Frame (among others) came to view Van Til as too "militant" in contending for the faith. At this point in the history of the seminary, faculty members were eager to forge new ground, even if theological explorations countered traditional, confessional teaching. This became full blown with the dispute swirling around the views of systematics professor Norman Shepherd in the mid-1970s. Pivotal in this controversy was Shepherd's doctrine of justification by faith (and works), election as losable, and his repudiation of the classic Reformed doctrine of the Covenant of Works. It would be several years later before the doctrine of the "republication" of the Covenant of Works under Moses (the legal covenant republished *in modified form*) would move to the center. Proper interpretation of the works-inheritance principle operative in the old, Mosaic economy of redemption is the linchpin for the biblical exposition of the doctrine of justification by faith alone—giving expression to the traditional Law/Gospel antithesis (see, e.g., Acts 13:38–39). It is my contention that the doctrine of republication is, indeed, the view of mainstream Reformed theology.

This book concludes my lengthy analysis and critique of theological developments at Westminster Seminary, written with the hope and prayer that truth may yet come to full, undiminished light in Reformed theology and practice in our generation. Covenant theology, or "federalism," is the hallmark of the Reformed tradition. The closing Epilogue provides an overview of Reformed faith and practice from the perspective of the covenants God has made with his people.

Mark W. Karlberg
October 31, 2017
500th Anniversary of the Protestant Reformation

Section One

The Development of Doctrine in the History of the Church

Chapter One

The History of Doctrine
A Broad Overview

It would be a happy circumstance indeed were students of the Bible down through the ages of church history to agree on all matters pertaining to the interpretation of the Bible—at least on matters pertaining to the core doctrines of the Christian faith, those doctrines which stand at the center, rather than the periphery, of the system of doctrine laid out in holy Scripture. As it turns out, the mind of the church has not been in agreement on numerous subjects addressed in the Bible. Among the people of God, controversy and conflict appear over the course of biblical history, notably, in the history of the ancient Israelite theocracy, as well as in the early life of the Christian church subsequent to the Day of Pentecost—when the Spirit of God was poured out upon the whole church for the purpose of the spread of the Gospel, for the attainment of true unity among the saints, and for genuine conviction of the truth of God's Word. Since the time of the Protestant Reformation, never have the Reformed churches been in more theological disarray than at present. Is the church entering another Dark Age?

The promise of the pentecostal Spirit has reference—among other concerns—to the gradual appropriation of God's truth in the hearts and minds of believers, most immediately to the apostles and writers of the new covenant scriptures, whose teachings were wholly inspired. Whether we consider the elucidation of the Word of God by these writers or by theologians in the subsequent history of the Christian church, the proclamation of divine truth always requires its *polemical* defense. Assuredly, Christian doctrine is forged in the fires of debate and controversy. The apostle Paul

Section One: The Development of Doctrine

challenged the Galatian judaizers who sought to pervert his teaching concerning free justification (justification by grace through faith, apart from the works of the law). Likewise, the early church confronted head-on the heresy of gnosticism and other similar threats upon the faith, which is the sacred tradition now handed down from the apostles of Christ to succeeding generations of faithful Christians.

The history of doctrine—or what is known as the discipline of historical theology—shows the gradual, progressive apprehension of the teachings of the Bible in the mind of the church. There is not only progressive development, but also retrogression in understanding through misinterpretation and perversion of the truth.[1] The early church, for example, addressed challenges to the doctrine of the triunity of God, the full deity and humanity of Christ as incarnate Son of God, and the continuity of divine revelation under the two economies of redemption (the Mosaic and the new covenant). These controversies resulted in the writing of the so-called "ecumenical" creeds of the church, statements of faith which continue to represent the teaching of orthodox, biblical Christianity. These include the Nicene, the Chalcedonian, and the Athanasian Creeds, documents that stand as testaments of faith, milestones in the history of Christian interpretation. In some instances these confessional formulations require additional modification or clarification. (It is to be observed, some communities of faith read alien notions into the creedal statements—hence the need for additional commentary and clarification.) The Spirit of God truly leads the church into the truth of the Scriptures, more exactly, into the true *apprehension* of God's inscripturated revelation. Oftentimes it requires theological controversy to raise questions and issues never before raised or adequately addressed in the history of the church doctrine. Only then is the mind of the church pressed to probe more deeply into the teachings of the Bible—with a degree of intensity unprecedented in former times.

The Early Church

The ancient church is divided between the Eastern fathers, who wrote in Greek, and the Western fathers, who wrote in Latin. (Hence, the division

---

1. There are no "new ideas" to arise in the history of biblical interpretation, in the sense of new light or new truth. The truth of God has been fully revealed in the Scriptures as a completed body of teaching. There is only growth in the church's *apprehension* of the Word.

is oftentimes classified as that between the Greek and Latin fathers.) Together, these theologians of the early church labored to enunciate—catholic and orthodox—what is biblical teaching expounded in opposition to views deemed heterodox in Greek and Roman philosophy and society more generally.[2] Contention for the true faith was not a simple or easy matter. Struggles were intense, oftentimes leading to severe persecution in the cross-fires of powerful political aspirants of the day. Ancient Christian society was largely theonomic in its outlook, the consequence of melding together two institutions that in Scripture are carefully distinguished. The two divinely ordained institutions are that of the church and the state. (It would take several centuries after the Protestant Reformation for right understanding and needed clarification of this biblical distinction to occur among [some] Protestant-Reformed interpreters of the Bible. Even at the opening of the twentieth century, the prospect of reaching a clear, unambiguous consensus on this subject is very far from reach.[3])

As partially a product of cultural and social factors, the formulation of Christian doctrine over the course of church history can and does convey at times unwelcome baggage. Certainly old, once settled opinions and viewpoints are difficult to change. Too often interpreters of the Bible, consciously or unconsciously, resist the convicting, teaching ministry of the Holy Spirit as he bears witness to the Christ of Scripture (and the whole counsel of God). Hardness of heart remains a constant threat to the life and well being of the church. The particular challenger to biblical exposition in the church in its earliest days was Hellenism, what was the dominant world-view in Greco-Roman culture and society, a world-view that was antagonistic to the biblical religion of the Old and New Testaments. Pagan religion, ancient or modern, is inherently syncretistic, a melding of diverse ideas and conceptualizations. Biblical religion, on the other hand, is unified and consistent, expressive of the eternal will and revelation of God made known in Christ Jesus. The church's interpretation of the Scriptures at the outset of the new economy of redemption, since the establishment of the new covenant in Christ's blood and extending to the close of church history at the end of the present eschatological

---

2. The earliest group of Christian writers after the close of the canon of Scripture are known as the "Apologists," appropriately named, in that they saw their chief purpose in the defense of the teachings of the Bible against contemporary threats and challenges.

3. See my "Reformation Politics: The Relevance of Old Testament Ethics in Calvinist Political Theory," *JETS* 29 (1986) 179–91, republished in Karlberg, *Covenant Theology in Reformed Perspective*; and "Westminster and Washington: Church and State in American Calvinism," in Karlberg, *Federalism and the Westminster Tradition*.

Section One: The Development of Doctrine

age, entails the progressive, ongoing *appropriation* of God's revealed truth contained in his Word and in nature (otherwise known as general revelation in distinction from special revelation), and the repudiation of foreign, speculative notions that have gained false entrance into the church's articulation of her faith (i.e., church doctrine or "dogma").

Despite obstacles and difficulties awaiting biblical interpreters in the span of time between the first and second comings of Christ, great strides were made in the early church, and continue to be made throughout church history. From the earliest days, Christians acknowledged the uniqueness and authority of the canon of Scripture, Old and New, even if there was some confusion regarding the precise list of books comprising the sacred writings. As a theological conclusion, the canonicity of Scripture was the result of the providential working of the Spirit of God in the mind and hearts of believers, not the result of church counsels or human deliberation acting on the basis of external criteria deemed essential for biblical canonicity. The (Protestant) church's final position on the canonical books of the Bible came as a result of the Spirit's illumination and conviction among the faithful in the earliest centuries of church history and again in the time of the Protestant Reformation. This was the outworking of God's sovereignty and providence. In every respect he is the lord and protector of the church and of her inspired, sacred writings.

The first major challenge to the church's received text was made by Marcion, who based his list of New Testament books on his own peculiar and heretical assessment of the God of the Old Testament. This god, claimed Marcion, was opposite to the god of love portrayed in the New Testament. Here we find a clear instance of an alien world-view and hermeneutic functioning in the interpretation of the Bible. A particular human philosophy of things divine is imposed upon the reading of Scripture. Another movement in the early church that threatened the authority of the Word was that of Montanism. The modern phenomenon of pentecostalism has its roots in an allegedly "ecstatic (spiritual) experience" of revelation. Simply stated, the assumption is made that in this present age of the church the Spirit of God directly—apart from the inscripturated Word—illumines the human mind concerning divine truth ("special" revelation). Personal experience—or the inner light as taught in Quakerism[4]—is the ultimate criterion in the discernment of truth.

---

4. There are evangelical brands of Quakerism today, but these are radical modifications of an earlier religious tradition. Even so, the soundness of this eclectic version evangelicalism, one of many, can be fairly questioned.

The History of Doctrine

In the history of philosophy the same kind of subjectivism became dominant in the thinking of twentieth-century theologian Friedrich Schleiermacher. In his wake many modern theologies build on subjectivism—a view that in certain respects is the climax of Enlightenment rationalism.

Hermeneutics is the science of the interpretation of the Bible. It is as old as Christianity. Even the inspired writers of Scripture employed a hermeneutic. In their case it was divinely instilled—and at the same time based upon the infallible and inerrant Scriptures. According to the later Reformed tradition, the biblical hermeneutic is *the self-authenticating Christ speaking through the Scriptures*. Biblical truth (as it has been passed down to us in the Christian church) is based upon a closed canon, and it is also opposed to alien notions dominant in the secular culture. This conviction concerning the inscripturated Word does not undermine the fact that special and general revelation complement one another. That said, general revelation (in the world and in human conscience) cannot be rightly understood apart from special revelation. The relationship between these two forms of revelation—including the modern subject of the relationship between science and the Bible—remains yet another subject of discussion and debate over the course of the history of Christian interpretation.

A classic writing of Augustine, the greatest of the Latin fathers, was entitled *The City of God*. Here Augustine surveyed the history and philosophies of two antithetical cities, the city of God and the city of man. The city of God was built and nurtured upon Christ and his authoritative Word; the city of man was a counterfeit imitation, seductive and self-destroying. It was Augustine's predecessor, Tertullian, who described the contrast of philosophies as that between Jerusalem and Athens, between the heavenly realm and the realm of secular humanism (i.e., humanistic rationalism). What does Jerusalem have to do with Athens, asked Tertullian? Today Christian interpreters continue to debate this same question. Answers cover an exceedingly wide spectrum of opinion. The temptation to dress God's Word in the cloak of humanistic thinking and to subject the teachings of the Bible to human standards of judgment remains a constant temptation and threat to the Christian church as a historical institution and entity living out its existence in "this present evil age" (Gal 1:4). Is Scripture truly and uniquely authoritative? Is Scripture alone the infallible and inerrant Word of God? These would be the critical questions the church would have to answer with increasing clarity over the passage of time.

SECTION ONE: THE DEVELOPMENT OF DOCTRINE

The earliest interpreters of the Bible gave clear articulation to the unity and diversity of special revelation over the course of biblical history, the history of redemption. Most important in this regard was the contrast between the old and the new economies of redemption, the Mosaic epoch and the Christian. Christ is both the midpoint and the climax of redemptive history; he is the center of world history, the fulfillment of the ancient promises first declared to Adam after his transgression in the Garden of Eden ("the seed of the woman"). We look especially to the Latin fathers for sound patterns of teaching concerning the relationship between the old and new covenants, and for typological interpretation of the two Testaments (these two subjects are bound together). Here the Latin fathers grasped far better than the speculative and allegorical Greek fathers the historical and prophetic nature of redemptive revelation in the time of the old economy, what was preparatory and propaedeutic for the establishment of the new, eternal covenant in Christ's blood poured out for many for the remission of sins. These students of the Bible understood well the organic relationship between the two epochs of revelation—from initial seed to full flowering. It was Augustine's hermeneutical distinction between "letter" and "Spirit" that further paved the way for Martin Luther's reclamation of the biblical doctrine of justification by faith alone in the time of the Protestant Reformation. There is only one way of salvation under two economies of redemption, old and new.

Tertullian, a lawyer turned theologian, was the first to introduce the term "merit" into the theological vocabulary. He and his fellow interpreters of Scripture, however, failed to understand the unique and radical nature of divine grace operative in the salvation of those who are in Christ Jesus. Saving, justifying grace is wholly antithetical to inheritance by works (human "merit"). Subsequent to Adam's fall, sinners are incapable of achieving their salvation by obedience to the law of God. The way of salvation is the way of faith, not works—it is the way of grace, not law (as a covenant of works). The dominant view of the day was that Christ is our moral example. As the new law-giver he has demonstrated for us the way of faith, hope, and love. According to this interpretation salvation is reduced to moralism, which says that one is to strive to do his best in love for God and neighbor. God is just and will reward the creature for his moral earnestness. This misinterpretation, or rather distortion, concerning the way of salvation has resurfaced time and again in the history of the Christian church, albeit with various mutations, some subtle and others overt. The biblical doctrine of justification by faith alone became the rallying cry of the Protestant Reformation, beginning in the sixteenth century. It has been called the doctrine of the standing church—the church standing on the testimony of Scripture, proclaiming the one and only gospel of sovereign, electing grace.

One of the greatest challenges in the early church was the Christian doctrine of the Trinity. Arianism, monarchianism, and a host of other heresies appeared on the scene undermining apostolic teaching. The gist of this controversy was the issue of unity and distinction within the Godhead, the eternal coexistence of three persons—equal in power, glory, and sovereignty, yet distinct in their relations and subsistence. The Father is not the Son; the Son is not the Spirit. Directly related was the question of subordination of persons within the Godhead. How does the biblical interpreter reconcile *apparently contrary and irreconcilable* teachings in the Bible? The classic doctrine of the triunity of the Godhead underscores the oneness of the divine persons. Here is mystery to be sure, revelation that transcends finite, human comprehension.

Here at the same time marks the beginning of the church's reflection on the doctrine of the infinitude and incomprehensibility of God, what in shorthand is the distinction between the Creator and the creature, between the infinite and the finite, a theme to which Christian interpreters would return time and again. Can the finite creature know truth *as God knows*? We confess that God himself is truth, and ask: Is God's image-bearer capable of being assimilated into the being and knowledge of God (God who reveals truth and is truth)? Is man's thoughts of what is true identical with that of God's? Can a "mystical" (ecstatic) experience transform the creature into the divine nature, whereby the two become one? The transformation of those renewed in the image of Christ has been variously described as deification, recapitulation, beatification, or glorification. Moving beyond mere terminology, we are obliged to consider the content of doctrinal formulation as that has come down to us in the history of Christian theology. What meaning is given to these terms?

Complicating matters epistemological and metaphysical in nature is the reality of sin within the human race. Not only finitude, but transgression and rebellion against the Creator impede our understanding of divine revelation. Humankind has fallen under the wrath and displeasure of God; sin has created a chasm between the creature and the Creator. Darkness has come upon humankind, and the mind is now blind to the things of God. Should Christ's redemptive work on the cross be viewed as a ransom to the Devil, or as payment for sin and satisfaction of divine justice? Clarity on these issues would also await the Protestant Reformation, when the medieval (notably, the Anslemic) view regarding legal satisfaction would ultimately prevail. In his atoning work Christ conquered death, rendering Satan powerless and defeated. The Spirit of Christ brings illumination and true of understanding of the Word.

Debates arose over the formulation of the two natures of Christ, the human and the divine. The "Word-flesh" and "Word-man" christologies competed with one another, only the latter doing fuller justice to the two distinct natures of Christ within the one person. Needless to say, the doctrine of the incarnation of the Son of God is foundational for understanding the redemption accomplished by Christ Jesus, the God-man and Second Adam. The Westminster divines in the seventeenth century would give eloquent, summary expression to this biblical teaching.

The doctrine of sin—including an understanding of the ramifications of sin for the cosmos in general and humanity in particular—is given meager attention in the early church. Prevailing thought merely accented the recapitulation or summing up of God's creative and re-creative work in the advents of Christ (first and second), centering upon Christ's decisive conflict with and defeat of Satan. The mystery of the birth of the human soul confounded biblical interpreters, leading them to two very different lines of thinking. Traducianism contends that the soul is borne alone through human procreation; creationism teaches that each human soul is created at conception. Equally mysterious is the origin and spread of sin within the human race. According to one view, the transmission of sin takes place solely through natural descent; according to another view, sin and guilt entails the imputation of original sin, Adam's first act of transgression in Paradise as the federal head of the human race.

As early as the apostolic church the threat of gnosticism loomed large in Christian circles. Is the essence of human personality spiritual or physical, or both? Is physical matter inherently evil, or to any degree tending toward unspiritualilty? Do practices of asceticism aid in the depredation of the body and the cultivation of the soul? Do we become more God-like by ascetic practices and divine contemplation, the two pillars of monasticism? Gnostic teaching calls into question both the necessity and efficacy of Christ's atonement, his physical death upon a wooden cross. Redemption, according to the gnostics, is the individual's gradual (spiritual) elevation to the divine, heavenly realm by means of the purification of the mind and the assimilation of "secret" truths, truths revealed only to those initiated into the faith. Enlightenment is essentially an ecstatic experience.

The church's many battles over doctrine necessitated catechetical writing, wherein teaching deemed orthodox would be summarily formulated and methodically taught to new converts. From the earliest days, catechesis was a critically important tool in Christian nurture and in the extension of the true, apostolic faith throughout the world. (It remains a vital tool for each subsequent generation of believers. Neglect of catechetical instruction imperils the health and well-being of the church.)

The Medieval and Reformation Church

Somewhat surprisingly, the concept of covenant began to take on considerable importance in medieval theology. In large part, the impetus for this development was the prominence of political alliances or covenants throughout Europe. It was much the same in ancient Mesopotamia (at the time of Moses and the birth of the Israelite theocracy), when suzerainty treaties were commonplace. In the good providence of God, the sovereign Lord was pleased to enter into covenant with a special people—a people consecrated and made holy (set apart)—for the purpose of preparing the way for the coming of the Messiah, the Lord's Anointed. To be sure, covenants between God and his chosen saints were not new in the time of Moses, but appear already from the earliest of times. God was pleased to covenant anew with Adam after his fall into sin. This new covenant (what would later be termed "the Covenant of Grace" by Reformed theologians) was significantly different from the covenant God made with Adam at the opening of history (what came to be known as "the Covenant of Works").

What is important in this brief account of the history of Christian doctrine is the fact that medieval scholasticism became fixated upon the covenant which God had established with the church, the sacraments here viewed as the means for the extension of God's spiritual kingdom in the world. Sacramentalism is the doctrine that the church possesses the efficient means of dispensing redemptive grace (*ex operato*) to sinners who then are ingrafted into Christ (via baptism) and who commune regularly with the mystical body of God (via the eucharist, or "mass"). Church and covenant are inextricably bound together in medieval Christianity; sacerdotalism is the doctrine that the priests are the administrators and conveyers of the saving grace of God sacramentally dispensed to the church. This interpretation captures the essence of Roman Catholic ecclesiology.

Implicit in the sacramentalist understanding of the church is the importance and role given to the clerics. A caste of priestly mediators was devised whereby Christ's redemptive work on earth was thought to be extended through such intermediaries as Mary, the mother of our Lord Jesus Christ, and through the papal system. Martin Luther would challenge this false doctrine in his call for the priesthood of all believers. According to Luther, there is only one mediator between God and the sinner, Jesus Christ. In Christ, we are all priests and prophets ministering the grace of God to needy sinners by Word and witness. In conjunction with the Roman understanding of the church's sacraments is the medieval, scholastic doctrine that God rewards those who do their very best. Salvation is viewed to be a cooperative enterprise between God and the creature endowed with freedom of the will. Contrary to Augustinian-Reformed theology, sin does not negate human ability, but merely makes the pilgrim's path to salvation a bit more difficult to attain. The essential contours of Roman Catholic soteriology were laid in the early church, most notably in the debate between Augustine, who anticipated many of the doctrines associated with Reformed Protestantism, and Pelagius, the father of Arminian theology. It is fitting, the scholastics taught, that God would reward the best efforts of the *viator* (the Christian pilgrim) in conjunction with the merits of Christ's obedience unto death. According to Rome, salvation is a matter of faith and works.

Two kinds of merit were now introduced into the theological vocabulary, teaching that would become deeply imbedded and conflicted in Christian thought for generations to come. The first was "strict" merit (also called condign merit); Christ's righteousness was seen as having intrinsic, meritorious value. From one perspective, Christ alone merits the salvation of sinners. On the grounds of his meritorious and vicarious (i.e., substitutionary) obedience, salvation was won for transgressors of the law of God. The second kind of merit was termed "congruent merit"; the sinner's good works (his less than perfect righteousness) is accepted by God on the basis of divine generosity. The best efforts of the saint are *added* to the merits of Christ in the procurement of individual salvation. The doctrine of acceptation is based upon the "half-merits" of observing God's law and availing oneself of the grace bestowed by the church upon the faithful through the sacraments. This doctrine of salvation attributes more worth to human works than they

The History of Doctrine

inherently possess. Again, it is the combination of human works (even those defiled by sin) and sacramental grace that earns eternal life.

The doctrine of the covenant also gave further justification in the minds of the scholastic medievalists for the union between church and state as two divinely-ordained institutions whose purpose was to defend and maintain the Christian faith throughout all of Christendom (hence, the union of the two kingdoms, the spiritual and the temporal). Whatever tensions arose between the heads of state and the head of the church, the pope, in their respective quest for primacy, those conflicts were secondary to the importance of maintaining the role of the civil magisterium in the promotion and extension of the Christian faith, even by use of the sword. The medieval notion of "Christendom" would last well into the twentieth century.[5]

The Protestant Reformation—including the post-Reformation epoch—cannot be properly assessed or understood apart from the background provided by medieval scholasticism, particularly the movement known as nominalism. Though diverse in its history and teaching, nominalism was largely the amplification of scholastic teaching on the cooperative effect of congruent and condign merit in the salvation of sinners—sinners saved by divine grace and human works (= synergism). Virtually all of the themes of the Reformation were drawn from medieval theology, though many were recast in distinctly Protestant categories. The above discussion already intimates many of the issues and concerns that were to be raised and debated in the sixteenth and seventeenth centuries, the formative period of Protestant-Reformed Orthodoxy viewed as a whole.

Impacting the Reformed doctrine of the covenants is the biblical teaching concerning the sovereign decrees of God in election and reprobation. Three pivotal doctrines in the Reformed arsenal in the Reformation/post-Reformation age are these: justification by faith (alone), the covenants (works and grace), and decretive election. To be sure, Reformed theology cannot be reduced to these three points of doctrine, any more than it can be reduced to the famous "five points of Calvinism" drawn up at the Synod of Dort in the early seventeenth century. Nevertheless, these elements of doctrine are highly determinative of Reformed theology, such that any radical recasting of these central doctrinal elements results in the betrayal and demise of confessional

---

5. Conflicting views on the relationship between church and state continue on into modern-day discussion and debate. But for the most part, the idea of "Christendom" is a thing of the past, especially in this post-Christian era in which we now live.

Section One: The Development of Doctrine

Reformed orthodoxy—so formative was Reformation teaching in the history of doctrinal theology (more precisely, church dogmatics).

More than anything else, the Reformation movement was a return to the teachings of the Word of God, brought about by the providential working of God's Spirit, the one who brings truth to light and instills conviction in the mind and heart of those regenerated. The return to the Bible did not entail, as is often thought, a disregard for churchly tradition, medieval or ancient. What was required was careful sifting of the church's received doctrines. *Tradition was subordinate to—not on a par with—the teachings of Scripture.* To the extent that the dogmas of the church were reflective of biblical doctrine they are to be believed and obeyed. The Reformation understanding of the doctrine of Scripture did not result in bibliology (the worship of the Bible), but rather in the recognition that the Bible was indeed what is truly conveys, namely, the authoritative, infallible (and inerrant) revelation God inscripturated, breathed out by the Spirit of God upon human authors. One of the slogans of the Reformation was *sola scriptura*: Scripture is self-interpreting and self-authenticating. This is the first and formal principle of Scripture (comprising what is known as the *theological prolegomenon*, "first things").

The Protestant-Reformed doctrine of the Bible called into question the role and significance of philosophy as the handmaid of theology (as commonly understood in prior ages). "Critical use" of philosophical reasoning (that which gives priority to human reason, above the divine Logos) resulted in the undermining of the teaching of Scripture. The development of a distinctly Reformed science of hermeneutics would be honed over the course of time. But for starters, a radical break was made with so-called "natural theology." The initial fruit of the reassessment of the relationship between philosophy and theology was part and parcel of the introduction to the topic of prolegomena, first-principles in the interpretation of the Bible, principles drawn from Scripture itself. The subject of prolegomenon had now become a distinct and vital locus within the system of Protestant-Reformed dogmatics. In brief: it is thinking God's thoughts after him (as revealed in nature and Scripture). Church theology is ectypal of truth as it is in the mind of God (the archetype). Recognizing the distance between the finite (man) and the infinite (God), man's thoughts are never identical to God's. To know precisely as God knows would mean that man is somehow *divinized* in the process of knowing himself and the world.

Perhaps the greatest achievement of the age of the Reformation was the degree of consensus reached within confessional Protestantism. Though there were a number of important doctrinal differences between the two main branches of evangelicalism, Lutheran and Reformed, they paled in comparison to what these two traditions shared in common. Our account of Christian theology, however, focuses upon the distinctive contribution of the Reformed or Calvinistic tradition, viewed in terms of its systematic integrity, consistency and coherence of biblical truth. Of course, this theological tradition has learned much from others, and will continue to do so as long as it seeks to be *reformed and being reformed according to the Word of God*. The epitome of Reformed Christianity is found in the writing of the Westminster Confession of Faith (and its accompanying catechisms, the Shorter and the Larger). Here is Reformed Orthodoxy in its fullest, most comprehensive statement, a testimony to the enduring legacy of the age of the Reformed Protestantism.

With respect to the system of doctrine, the capstone is eschatology—teaching concerning the consummation of God's initial, creative plan and purpose first introduced in the Book of Genesis. Perhaps surprisingly, this locus of doctrine was not fully developed (or rather fully integrated into the system of doctrine) in the Reformation period. Nevertheless, important and determinative insights were laid for future generations of Reformed interpreters. *The doctrine of the covenant would prove to be the linchpin in grasping the overarching design, as well as the historical unfolding, of God's spiritual kingdom in the midst of the nations of the world.* And it was the doctrine of eschatology that gave rise to Christian missions as we have come to know it in the modern world. The "Puritan hope" or expectation of things to come was largely instrumental in arousing the church to deepen its mission outreach, outreach that would eventually transform global Christianity. And in its wake came renewed attempts to define the proper, biblical relationship between church and state, and church and society.

The Modern Church

The modern age opens with the arrogant and defiant claim—an echo of the ancient philosophers—that "man is the measure of all things." And so this age, like every age in the postlapsarian world, is one of conflict as well as growth and change. Since the days of the Enlightenment movement, the hot topic of hermeneutics has moved to the front burner, being continuously watched and stirred. It is but the latest chapter in the history of the opposition between Jerusalem and Athens, the city of God and the city of man. The new feature in this modern period is the advent of higher criticism as a newly crafted discipline in the study of world religions in particular and of the humanities in general. Modernist "higher criticism" applies to the sacred writings the same vigorous, "scientific" principles of investigation that have come to define enlightened, autonomous man. No longer can it be assumed or presupposed that the Bible is the Word of God. Modernist critics approach the writings of the Old and New Testaments as purely "secular" documents, writings arising out of the universal, common religious experience shared by all peoples, albeit in different and sometimes competing cultures and by very different mind-sets. Enlightenment dogma epitomizes the spirit of modernist thought (including what is now called "foundationalism," a term descriptive of the attempt to base truth on a foundational, rational principle of human epistemology). Truth is ascertained on purely scientific grounds, by a methodology which recognizes the autonomy of human reason. (Non-foundationalism, as a recent-day, reactionary philosophical school of thought, claims that all theologizing and philosophizing is relative in nature; interpretation depends upon one's place in history and culture. Consequently, truth in the minds of each and every individual is elusive and ever-changing. Some contend that divine revelation itself is ever in flux; others espouse a more traditional understanding of ultimate truth as that which is contained in the mind of God, not in the minds of men. In the final analysis, foundationalism and nonfoundationalism are half-brothers).

Relentless application of the Enlightenment hermeneutic results in the practice of demythologization, best exemplified in the work of existentialist theologian Rudolf Bultmann. Biblical stories undergo reinterpretation according to the canons of modern, rationalistic science. Myth is removed from what is considered to be merely ordinary human experience; the supernatural element is extracted altogether from the witness of Scripture. Accounts of the absolute creation of heaven and the earth, miracles, and special providence all lose their biblical meaning and veracity. At the same time attention now turns to the history and message of Jesus of Nazareth, the "new quest" for the historical Jesus. Christianity is most often reduced to moralism, and the scriptural documents are left to the judgment of redaction critics who freely speculate on their composition and on matters relating to authorial intent.

The History of Doctrine

The new secular humanism gave birth to three offspring: process theology (including "Open Theism"), liberation theology, and contextual theology.[6] New hermeneutical assumptions have produced startling reinterpretations of Christianity and the religions of the world. Rapprochement between the various religions is now taking place in full earnest. This dominant, secular point of view has begun to impact evangelicalism in a way that calls into question the particularity of the gospel of Jesus Christ. The relationship between God and the world is reinterpreted in the light of the assimilation of the one with the other. Frequently, both are understood to be in the process of "becoming." In secular academia the very notion of Christianity as the true religion is no longer tenable (nor countenanced in many circles).

But the story does not end here. With the advent of the post-modern (or post-Christian) era, the time has seemingly come when old "assumptions"—as diverse as the inerrancy of Scripture and the reliability of the scientific approach to knowledge (i.e., foundationalism)—are cast aside in favor of a renewed appreciation for the formative role of the believing community in the universal quest for truth. Truth has come to be defined in terms of religious practice and communal values. Conservative evangelical theology (both Reformed and non-Reformed varieties) now appear as reactionary and antiquated. Within the Evangelical Theological Society, illustrative of the state of post-modern evangelicalism, the foundational doctrine of biblical inerrancy has been sidelined by the plethora of interpretations vying for acceptance among the theologians of the church. Disdain for traditional systematic theology has led to the heightened appeal for narrative theology, an approach to the Bible which grants the community of faith a creative and determinative role in the (ongoing) articulation of Christian doctrine. Here the preferred concept is the "drama" of doctrinal teaching. Christian doctrine is no longer seen as the restatement of the teachings of the Bible in the socio-historical context of changing times and divergent cultures. Truth is what is true for the community of faith, relative to its place in history. Granted, there is often a positive appreciation for confessional theology, but this is undermined by the assumption that all theological discourse is, in the final analysis, relative and contextual. There

---

6. Contextualization is altogether different from communicating the message of Scripture in difficult cultures and different societies. Contextual theology, what purports to be a new hermeneutical approach based upon an experiential appropriation/application of the biblical text, reshapes the teaching of the Scriptures in terms of prevailing cultural ideas. This method of interpretation distorts, rather than illumines, the message of the Bible.

Section One: The Development of Doctrine

can be no equation of churchly dogma, we are told, with biblical truth. Neither of the two shall meet; they can only approximate one another—however weakly and tentatively. *The older Protestant understanding contends that to the degree that the confessional statements teach what is substantiated in Scripture, to that degree they are to be believed and obeyed. Such conviction of the truth, the reformers believed, is the result of the inward testimony of the Spirit of God.* We are now told that that point of view is no longer adequate or acceptable.

Other theological conflicts have likewise taken their heavy toll on evangelical churches in the modern period. These include Pentecostalism, with its free-Spirit, and dispensationalism, with its cut-and-paste method in interpreting biblical history and teaching. How do these developments in theology impact Reformed Christianity in particular? In some circles renewed interest in the doctrines of eschatology and the covenants has called for a return to the theological heritage of historic Calvinism. But with respect to the rise and development of scholastic Reformed Orthodoxy (also known as "federalism"), there is no lack of defenders and detractors, both sides claiming to speak on behalf of genuine, authentic Calvinism. Radically divergent interpretations of the covenants in Scripture compete today even within "confessional" Reformed theology. Who are the faithful interpreters of the tradition of Calvin and his (true) successors? The opinions to this question are legion. In addition, there are those who advocate Christian Reconstructionism (otherwise known as "theonomy"), those who advocate a form of narrative theology which recognizes some of the themes in traditional covenant theology (including the interplay between covenant and eschatology), and those who portray Calvinism as the nemesis of Lutheranism regarding the crucial subject of the relationship between Law and Gospel. The health of the Reformed churches stands in great jeopardy today, and will continue to do so as long as these issues are left unresolved or conflicted.

Throughout the course of the history of doctrine, Reformed covenant theologians have sought to bring together into a systematic whole the various threads of biblical teaching as presented in Scripture's grand mosaic. Implicitly, the theology of the covenants is both systematic and biblical-historical, the latter methodological approach emphasizing the progressive unfolding of redemptive revelation in biblical history. If the history of doctrine tells us anything, it tells us that Christian doctrine must be reformed and reforming according to the Word of God. That task remains until the return of Christ in consummate Glory. Modern-day princes of Reformed interpretation include the great stalwarts of the faith who taught at Princeton Seminary in the nineteenth and early twentieth centuries. Their work was faithfully and vigorously carried on by the first-generation faculty of Westminster Seminary, including exponents of orthodox Calvinism in the Netherlands, one of the few remaining strongholds of the Reformed faith in Europe. Among the notable theologians of Dutch extract who would later become prominent in America are Louis Berkhof, Herman Bavinck, Geerhardus Vos, and Cornelius Van Til. Reformed churches committed to historic Calvinism continue stand in their debt.

Concluding Thoughts: The Threat of Heresy

The criterion of truth is Scripture, Scripture alone. But the church's (fallible) understanding of what Scripture teaches over the entire course of church history is subject to ongoing study, discussion, and debate. As we will see in Chapters Two and Three, it is the Spirit of illumination who guarantees true appropriation of God's Word by those who have been sanctified in the truth (see John 17:17). The individual conscience, as illustrated in the case of Martin Luther in his opposition to the teachings of Rome and in his defense of the pure, unadulterated teaching of Scripture, is bound to God and his Word, free from human doctrine and opinion (compare *WCF* 20.2). When and where there is consensus of opinion among faithful ministers and teachers in Christ's church, the statement of doctrine in confessional form is necessary for the church's health and well-being. Churchly dogma is valid only to the extent that it faithfully and accurately restates the teaching of the Bible. Ongoing restatement is all the more necessary in light of the church's progressive (and retrogressive) apprehension and understanding of what Scripture teaches. Confessional, dogmatic theology also renders essential service to the church by demarcating the boundaries of human inquiry and statements of faith, to the best of its ability and as determined by Scripture alone. Those doctrines which clearly fall outside the bounds of confessional orthodoxy are deemed *heretical*.

Dogmatician Otto Weber rightly identifies heresy as "the constantly threatening temptation" to pervert the Word of God. "Heresy is present *in nuce* wherever the Church in its proclamation makes a given or inherited human self-understanding into the criterion of the Word." Weber added: "Invariably this happens with the best of intentions: to mitigate the strangeness of the proclaimed Word, to make it easier for the listener to find access to the Word, to make it possible for the believer to exist in 'his' world. We must state, in fact, that the Church's proclamation can never avoid this *danger*."[7] Heresy is real—it is an ever-present threat. Above all, humility and care must be exercised by the church, by every student of the Bible, in the articulation and restatement of what Scripture teaches. Surely, the church's theological task bears a corporate dimension; theology is done in and among the community of the faithful in all ages of its history.

---

7. Weber, *Foundations of Dogmatics*, 24.

Chapter Two

Theological First-Principles
The Why and How of Thinking Biblically

STUDY OF THE BIBLE requires us to begin by asking some basic, foundational questions—questions that impact how we interpret the Bible. Before all else we must ask: How do we know? This question concerns epistemology. There is no more basic or preliminary issue than this. Contrary to the teaching of many, the human mind is not a blank tablet to which are added various presuppositions and assumptions, adopted volitionally (or non-volitionally) by the knowing inquirer. The apostle Paul plainly teaches that all men do know that God exists and that he rewards those who keep his commandments, while condemning those who transgress his law. However, the apostle acknowledges that to one degree or another sinners, given their depraved nature (the consequence of the sin of our first federal head, Adam), *suppress the truth in unrighteousness.* Views of God, the world, and oneself are distorted and, at best, partially true. Not only is the mind darkened, the will is likewise bound to sin and cannot please God (apart from spiritual regeneration). Reconciliation between creature and Creator and restoration to life with God requires the sovereign, gracious initiative of God in the salvation of sinners. Conviction of sin and the truth of divine revelation both in nature and in Scripture are the fruits of the Holy Spirit's restorative work—regenerating, indwelling, and illuminating.

Sinners, regenerate and unregenerate alike, may have ready access to the sacred writings, the Old and New Testaments. By common grace (a gift *graciously* bestowed upon all humankind) they have the ability to read and assimilate, to some extent, the teaching of the Bible. The godly can learn from the ungodly in the interpretation and explanation of what the Bible teaches. The difference resides in the fact that only the godly—those who have been renewed and sanctified—have *saving knowledge* of the truth of God as applied by the Spirit of Christ. "Faith comes from hearing, and hearing by the word of Christ" (Rom 10:17). The truth of Scripture is validated by the self-attesting Christ who speaks in Scripture, Old and New Testaments. It is confirmed in the hearts and minds of believers by the inward testimony of Christ's Spirit, the Spirit of God, the Spirit of illumination.

So too, the way one approaches Scripture and one's attitude toward the Bible wholly differs between the righteous and the unrighteous, between believer and unbeliever (including the skeptic). As Anselm stated long ago, "faith seeks understanding." The godly person believes in order to understand. *He thinks God's thoughts after the pattern of God's own self-revelation.* Biblical hermeneutics, the science or discipline of interpreting the Bible, is circular in nature. Students of the Bible enter this theological circle—comprising all the various and complementary theological sub-disciplines (e.g., exegesis, systematic and historical theology)—at any point in the trajectory and engage the entire corpus of teaching gleaned by the community of faith over the course of many centuries. Biblical affirmations and statements of doctrine serve as working presuppositions applicable to each and every discipline with the "theological encyclopedia," as it is comprehensively called. The introduction of any alien principle, hermeneutic, or doctrine results in misunderstanding and misconception. The community of faithful scholars (sound Christian scholarship at some level ought to be the aspiration of every believer) provides needed checks and balances for each particular, gathered community in any given generation, and over the span of generations. Ultimately, it is the Spirit of God who ensures genuine, lasting appropriation of God's Word. From the standpoint of the history of Christian doctrine there are seasons of progression, digression, and even retrogression in understanding. The task given to the church to pursue truth as revealed in the Bible continues on until the close of the age, the consummation of redemptive history and the inauguration of God's eternal purposes in Christ Jesus.

The Analogy of Scripture

The Reformed wing of the Protestant Reformation has identified Scripture itself as the first or formal principle in the revolution that was taking place in sixteenth-century Christian theology. It is the principle of *sola scriptura*—Scripture alone and in its entirety, the conduit of divine wisdom and understanding imparted to finite creatures (now fallen), God's image-bearers. The Bible is the Word of God, uniquely and authoritatively. It stands independent of all churchly tradition. However, to the extent that Christian tradition conveys the system (the pattern of truth) and doctrines set forth in the Bible, to that extent Christian tradition is of permanent, lasting duration—until we no longer see through a glass darkly (1 Cor 13:12). Less clear passages of Scripture are to be interpreted in the light of clearer passages. There is a completeness and coherence among the many and various strands of biblical teaching, some of it conveyed in prose and poetry, some in the form of metaphor, parable, and simile. Comprehensively speaking, biblical exegesis requires *literary-historical,* as opposed to merely grammatical-historical, interpretation. The exegete must understand the *genre* of sacred writing—be it narrative, poetic, or didactic.

Included in the implementation of the Scripture principle is acknowledgment that Scripture interprets Scripture. *The Word of God is self-interpreting and self-authenticating.* We do not find "proofs" of divine veracity outside of Scripture. (To be sure, there are many evidences of the divinity of Scripture within the pages of the Bible, just as there are many evidences and confirmations of historical and cosmic events cited in the Bible, evidences that may be obtained through study of the sciences, e.g., astronomy, geology, anthropology, and archeology. True science does not conflict with the teachings of the Bible; general and special revelation complement one another.) The rich diversity of God's revelation in Scripture and in nature in no way militates against its unity. In God the one and the many subsist. This is reflected in the Godhead itself, one God in three Persons. The finite mind is not capable of comprehending these truths, except by way of the analogy of Scripture (the analogy of faith). Christian theology has rightly maintained that Scripture is the ectype of truth, truth being God himself (the archetype). *All divine revelation is accommodated to finite human understanding. We know after a manner of speaking; we do not know as God knows.* The finite would have to be divinized in order to possess the same knowledge God has of his creation. Human knowledge is analogical—not equivocal—to God's knowledge. The two are not identical, and the difference is not merely the quantity of things known. Nevertheless, what we are granted to know is genuine and true. All that is impure and corrupted is false, the fruit of a clouded, rebellious mind that by nature is in opposition to the revelation of God's Word, fully revealed in the person and work of Jesus Christ (see John 1).

Rationalism is the belief that human and divine knowledge are identical. The fact that two plus two equals four is a datum of knowledge that God and intelligent creatures presumably share in common. The acquisition of enough "facts," arranged in proper (rational and logical) order, allegedly is capable of proving whatever confronts the human inquirer. Fideism, oftentimes contrasted with rationalism, is the exercise of faith in spite of (reasonable) evidence. The biblical doctrine of analogical human knowledge is neither fideistic (in this sense), nor rationalistic. True knowledge locates truth in God himself, not in the "bare" facts of the universe. God is the absolute Creator and the absolute knower, the only true interpreter and preserver of his created universe. In him—the eternal and all-glorious one and many—all truth resides. Man the creature is wholly dependent upon God for all things, including true knowledge, righteousness, and holiness (the original gifts to Adam prior to the Fall). Partial truths acquired by the ungodly are, in the words of twentieth-century Reformed apologist Cornelius Van Til, "borrowed capital" from true religion and revelation. Total darkness (the experience of hell) is the deprivation of all knowledge, righteousness, and holiness experienced by the sons and daughters of God (remade in God's image). Reformed hermeneutics seeks to bring every thought captive to the Word of God (2 Cor 10:5).

Sin and Its Consequences

Original sin, the offense of the First Adam resulting in human guilt and depravity, not only mars human knowledge of God, the world, and oneself, but also impedes the very process of acquiring knowledge. Obstacles arise that were not originally there in the created order of things. In the fallen world neither general nor special revelation can be rightly and truly received apart from the regenerating and illuminating work of the Spirit of God. Faith gives rise to understanding. The same Spirit who illumines our sinful minds also convicts and convinces us of the truth of God's Word (see 1 Cor 1–2). Man the creature, though fallen, ever remains entirely dependent upon God for revelation of his truth. In the wise and good providence of God the inscripturated Word comes to us as a record and testimony of God's saving work and grace, an account that is infallible and inerrant.

Theological First-Principles

All too frequently the assumption is made that at the very beginning, before the Fall, God's condescension in manifesting himself to Adam, son of God (bearer of God's image), was an act of divine *"grace."* More specifically, the covenant relationship established between God and Adam, federal representative of the entire human race, is viewed as a *gracious* arrangement. Here the speculative, rationalistic dichotomy between nature and grace—a theological commonplace in medieval scholasticism—rears its head. Consistently worked through the system of biblical doctrine, this notion of divine grace in the original order of creation ultimately leads to the denial of the Second Adam's meritorious accomplishment of redemption, the substitute for Adam's "one act of transgression" imputed to all humankind. (Some revisionists affirm the merit of Christ's substitutionary obedience rests on his unique deity and personhood. But their view cannot accommodate Paul's teaching in Romans 5 and elsewhere, teaching which posits a parallel between the "acts" of the First and Second Adams in their federal, representative capacities.) *Grace is God's remedy for sin and transgression of his covenant.* With respect to the universally received teaching of the Protestant Reformation—made explicit in the crucial distinction between the Law and the Gospel—the term "grace" is a purely *redemptive category*. There can be no admixture of law and (sovereign, electing) grace in the salvation of sinners. The speculative nature/grace (or nature/covenant) dichotomy has both epistemological and soteriological implications. One example is the rise of "natural theology," viewed as the foundation upon which supernatural revelation (grace) is built. Thomism is the classic example of this theological conceptualization. In soteriology, the nature/grace dichotomy results in the doctrine of two kinds of merit, condign and congruent. The first-generation reformers rejected this teaching, only to reappear (in somewhat modified, muted form) in Protestant scholasticism.

While biblical interpretation is a communal activity, it is also true that each believer has the responsibility to read, study, and meditate upon the Scriptures. We have but one teacher, the Holy Spirit. Church dogmas are to be received only if they are faithful restatements of the teaching of the Bible. Scripture and conscience are our guide. (Needless to say, church tradition does inform our judgment. But we must remember that the dogmatic confessions of the church, important as they are, stand as secondary norms for Christian faith and life.) The cultural mandate first given to humankind—the mandate to harness earth's resources and exercise universal dominion under God's sovereign rule—was a communal activity, having universal, global implications. Sin has introduced the bifurcation between cultic and cultural activities in the fallen world. (Church and state are two distinct, divinely-ordained institutions governing men and societies.) The sanctification of the redeemed people of God, the church of God under both dispensations of redemptive grace, has both individual and corporate dimensions. The impact of sin in the corporate structures of this world, including the institutionalization of the Christian church, necessitates the vigorous discipline and devotion of the saints of God to guard the faith once-for-all delivered to the saints, to withstand the evils (moral and doctrinal) of the present age in all its guises. There are occasions requiring a bold, courageous stand like that taken by Luther against erroneous teachings in the church, in witness to Scripture as the final rule of faith and practice. The reality and consequences of sin at work in the world and in the church underscore the importance and necessity of ongoing study, discipline, and nurture in the Word of God. Devotion to God requires devotion to his Word.

The Role of Confessionalism

The great creeds and confessions of the church are invaluable tools in the development, growth, and extension of the Christian faith throughout the world. The detail and depth of theological understanding progresses over time, and not always along a straight line. The earliest creeds of the church, the so-called ecumenical creeds, are recognized by both Catholic and Protestant communions. Yet, as the passage of time has shown all too clearly, these early statements of doctrine require amplification and clarification for the sake of clear understanding. The epitome of confessional writing in the age of Reformed Protestantism (at the middle of the seventeenth century) came with the writing of the Westminster standards, the Confession of Faith and the Larger and Shorter Catechisms. This survey of doctrine is written with the conviction that Reformed theology, expressed in the Westminster standards, is the most consistent and mature expression of biblical teaching in the Christian church to date. Reformed Christians are the bearers of a glorious tradition, yet one that recognizes the need for the church's ongoing reformation of doctrine in the light of the teaching of Scripture that comes over time. Dialogue with other Christian traditions, and non-Christian traditions, can serve to advance our understanding of Scripture (and its defense) and a better understanding of the world around us.

Though rarely understood or acknowledged, Reformed confessionalism seeks to set forth biblical teaching that speaks for orthodox Christianity at all times and in all places. It is not the objective of Reformed interpreters to (re)cast Scripture in a form or pattern of thought lacking the warrant of Scripture itself. Every theological tradition, by definition, conveys a particular "system" or method of doctrine, be it Reformed or Arminian, covenantal or dispensational, Word-centered or experience-centered (as in the case in Pentecostalism). Open, honest dialogue is the only means of attaining the unity of the faith that Scripture requires of all the faithful. Such unity is not optional, but necessary, for the vitality and strength of the church's public witness in the world. To be sure, perfect unity is not attainable in this present age. That awaits the Consummation, the radical in-breaking of God's eternal kingdom of righteousness and light. Until that time, we eagerly and earnestly seek truth in peace, unity, and purity.

Not coincidentally, the "rule of faith"—also called the analogy of Scripture—refers both to Scripture and to Christian tradition. Scripture alone is the absolute rule or norm; tradition (specifically, the confessions of the church) is the secondary norm of Christian faith. The interpretation of the Bible brings together Scripture and confession in mutual relationship. An error is often made when Scripture and church doctrine are held distinctly apart. The mistaken thinking here is the notion that the teaching of Scripture—denoted as "doctrine"—is distinct from churchly dogma—denoted as "theology". The implication is that theology is the (fallible) product of the church, whereas (pure) doctrine is peculiar to the content of Scripture itself. This view is based upon two misconceptions: (1) Scripture is thought to be devoid of *theological* exposition; and (2) post-canonical doctrine or theology is oftentimes mistakenly thought is be merely a *distant approximation* of biblical teaching. Some define "doctrine" as the straight-forward statements laid out in the Scriptures. As we have noted before, to the extent that Christian doctrine reflects the teaching of the Bible, to that extent it is to be believed and obeyed. Any lesser understanding of Christian doctrine relativizes all theological discourse in a way that undermines and undercuts the Protestant doctrine of the perspicuity of Scripture and the doctrine of the illumination of the Holy Spirit, which *guarantees* genuine appropriation of the truth of God's holy Word.

Section One: The Development of Doctrine

Presuppositionalism

No interpreter of the Bible approaches his or her task without some degree of preunderstanding (derived from various sources). Foremost within the faith community is confessional understanding imparted through the education and upbringing of parents and teachers, through literature and other educational media. Thus, each interpreter comes to Scripture with any number of presuppositions. What is required is that we examine and test each of these presuppositions in the light of the Scriptures. What are some of the basic presuppositions informing our interpretation of the Bible as a whole, presuppositions legitimized by the teaching of Scripture? They include belief that God is Creator and Lord; the Bible is the true Word of God; we are fallen creatures in need of repentance, regeneration, and renewal through the Spirit of God; the Holy Spirit himself is the ultimate interpreter of the inscripturated Word; the final judgment brings closure to God's creative/recreative purposes established in the person and work of his Son, the alone Savior from sin and its consequences.

The content of these presuppositional affirmations and principles of biblical interpretation is enlarged and deepened as one studies the Scriptures. The truth that God is triune is a mystery revealed supernaturally, by way of special revelation. The nature and consequences of the Fall—including the doctrine of probation and the imputation of sin and righteousness through the respective "acts" of the First and Second Adams—are comprehended incrementally (to the extent possible for the finite human mind). Over time the *elements of doctrine* find their place in the *system of doctrine* contained in Scripture. Theology, systematic and confessional, is the product of the Spirit's work of illumination among the community of the faithful. The saints of God appropriate divine truth by the inward testimony of the Spirit of God. Biblical presuppositionalism brings the teaching of Scripture to bear within the interpretive process. It is neither fideistic nor rationalistic. Biblical presuppositionalism grounds reason in Scripture, faith being the means of appropriating God's truth according to God's own self-revelation. Apart from faith, divine revelation cannot be properly or fully apprehended. Since humanity's fall into sin and darkness, faith is a gift of God's sovereign, electing grace. It is neither irrational nor fideistic, but rather authenticates human knowledge. Reformed epistemology requires the subjugation of all human thought to the counsel of God made known in Jesus Christ. Faith is neither blind trust, nor speculative (rationalistic), nor autonomous . In speaking of faith as that which authenticates knowledge, we are acknowledging that it is the Spirit of God who ultimately is the source of truth and illumination in human understanding.

Theology as a System of Doctrine

Perhaps the most hotly debated issue in contemporary hermeneutics is the traditional Protestant claim (one having full biblical justification) that Scripture and church theology, as a summary of what the Bible teaches, possess teaching that is systematically unified and coherent. Stated in other terms, the Protestant reformers have consistently maintained that the Bible contains a *system of doctrine*—a pattern of truth—that has been entrusted to the saints.[1] At no time in the history of Christian interpretation has this teaching been more vigorously refuted. Many contemporary theologians are persuaded that church theology is tentative and ever-changing. Absolute certainty of truth is beyond human attainment. Neo-Calvinist Gordon Spykman offers this assessment regarding the theological enterprise known as Reformed dogmatics: "This venture is therefore not motivated by some latter-day rationalist impulse for a closed system. Such theological imperialism would collapse under the sheer weight of its own intellectual arrogance. It is rather a matter of seeking to listen anew to the Word of God."[2]

John Frame's hermeneutical methodology, termed "multiperspectivalism," overturns centuries of Reformed interpretation by calling for an eclectic approach, one which homogenizes (at the same time that it relativizes) diverse theological discourse that has come to us through the long ages of church history.[3] More recently John Franke, after adopting the rationalistic assumption of nonfoundationalists, likewise challenges traditional views by denying there are any bed-rock, "foundational" principles which

---

1. Machen explains that theology "is a setting forth of those facts [of revelation] upon which experience is based. It is not indeed a complete setting forth of those facts, and therefore progress in theology becomes possible; but it may be true so far as it goes; and only because there is that possibility of attaining truth and of setting it forth ever more completely can there be progress" (*What is Faith?* 32–33). This subject has been helpfully taken up in a collection of essays by faculty members of Westminster Seminary entitled *The Pattern of Sound Doctrine: Systematic Theology at the Westminster Seminaries* (ed. David VanDrunen).

2. Spykman, *Reformational Theology*, 95.

3. See my critique of Frame's methodology: "On the Theological Correlation of Divine and Human Language," 99–105; "John Frame and the Recasting of Van Tilian Apologetics," 279–96; and "Fighting the Good Fight: A Bout with John Frame," 305–12.

can be apprehended with certitude. Nothing could be more foreign to the Protestant-Reformed understanding of Scripture and church tradition. Franke has worked in very close collaboration with Stanley Grenz. Franke's book, *The Character of Theology*, serves as a representative argument for the new "evangelical" school of thought. The heart of Franke's argument is this:

> The contextual nature of theology suggests the companion notion of theology as a second-order discipline and highlights its character as an interpretive enterprise. As such, the doctrinal, theological, and confessional formulations of theologians and particular communities are the products of human reflection on the primary stories, teachings, symbols, and practices of the Christian church. Therefore, these formulations must be distinguished from these "first-order" commitments of the Christian faith. For example, theological constructions and doctrines are always subservient to the content of Scripture and therefore must be held more lightly. In addition, the second-order nature of theology has entailed the development of conceptual vocabularies and sophisticated forms of argument that can appear to be far removed from idioms of Scripture.... The content of this theological metadiscourse should always be viewed as second-order, interpretive venture subject to further clarification, insight, and correction.[4]

By way of further amplification Franke adds that, "the task of theology in its various historical, cultural, ecclesial, and confessional contexts and expressions is to offer its particular witness to the Christian faith as an ecumenical enterprise for the purpose of contributing to the common task of the church to clarify the teaching of the one faith.... [T]he task of theology is critical and constructive reflection on the beliefs and practices of the Christian church. It suggests a model for theology that is inherently reforming in its openness to the Word of God and the multicultural Christian witness of the historical and global church and in keeping with the nature of theology as an ongoing, second-order, contextual discipline."[5]

What does this say about Scripture as the Word of God? Franke explains: "The assertion that our final authority is the Spirit speaking in and through Scripture means that Christian belief and practice cannot be determined merely by appeal either to the exegesis of Scripture carried out apart from the life of the believer and the believing community or to any 'word from the Spirit' that stands in contradiction to biblical exegesis. The

---

4. Franke, *The Character of Theology*, 104.
5. Ibid., 118.

THEOLOGICAL FIRST-PRINCIPLES

reading and interpretation of the text is for the purpose of listening to the voice of the Spirit, who speaks in and through Scripture to the church in the present."[6] What is Franke's distinction between the "primary teachings of the Bible" and churchly theology? Embracing the views of Stanley Hauerwas, Franke contends:

> [T]heological constructions and doctrines "are not the upshot of the stories; they are not the meaning or heart of the stories." Instead, they should be understood as tools whose purpose is to assist the community in hearing the Spirit's voice and "to help us tell the story better." Put another way, the task of theology is not an attempt to identify and codify the true meaning of the text in a series of systematically arranged assertions that then function as the only proper interpretive grid through which to read the Bible. Such an approach is characteristic among those who hold confessional statements in an absolutist fashion and claim that such statements teach the "system" of doctrine contained in Scripture. The danger here is that such a procedure can hinder the ability to read the text and to listen to the Spirit in new ways. Theology should always lead us back to the Bible. Its goal is to place the Christian community in a position to be receptive to the voice of the Spirit speaking in and through the biblical text to refashion the world after the eschatological mission and purposes of God. In light of this, the principle that the text of Scripture takes primacy over theological construction provides the basic parameter for understanding the interface between exegesis and theological reflection. If our working presupposition is not that the text exists primarily for the sake of theology but that theology serves the reading of the text, then we can no longer follow the commonly held view that the logical flow of Christian thought moves from biblical studies to a form of systematic theology. From this perspective, biblical scholars deliver to theologians the authentic biblical teachings in their unsystematic multiplicity, and theologians, in turn, bring these materials together into a systematic statement of what purports to be the doctrinal system taught in the Bible.[7]

The upshot of all this is that Franke drives a false wedge between Bible teaching ("the content of Scripture") and church theology. Consequently on this view, confessional Reformed dogmatics is relativized/contextualized in such a way that theology is no more than a speculative, rationalistic

---

6. Ibid., 131–32.
7. Ibid., 135.

enterprise in need of ongoing reformulation (but to what end?). Franke naively views exegesis as *pre-theological* reflection on what the Bible teaches. Were there any doubts where Franke is going in his thinking, we quote the following: "Viewed from the historical perspective, the Bible is the product of the community of faith that produced it. The compilation of Scripture occurred within the context of the faith community, and the biblical documents represent the self-understanding of the community in which they were developed." Not even Scripture is shielded from a historico-cultural hermeneutic that ends up in a relativistic sea of change. "What unifies this relationship between Scripture and the communal tradition of the church," writes Franke, "is the work of the Spirit. It is the Spirit who stands behind both the development and the formation of the community as well as the production of the biblical documents and their coming together into a single canon as that community's authoritative text. The community found these documents to be the vehicle through which they were addressed by the Spirit of God. The illuminating work of the Spirit brought forth these writings from the context of the community in accordance with the witness of that community. This work of illumination did not cease with the closing of the canon. Rather, it continues as the Spirit attunes the contemporary community of faith to understand Scripture and to apply it afresh to its own context in accordance with the intentions of the Spirit."[8]

Structure and Theme of the Divine Covenants

The biblical doctrine of God's covenants occupies a determinative place in our summary of Christian doctrine. This is not to suggest that "covenant" is the center or overarching theme of the Bible, even though it is an exceedingly important doctrine in the history of redemptive revelation, and in the theology of the Bible more generally. God does nothing apart from covenant; and all that he does in covenant is mediated by the Son, the eternal Logos. The triune God is the author of life and salvation. The heavens are upheld by his hand. Adam, God's image-bearer, was created in covenant relationship with God—Father, Son and Holy Spirit (the doctrine of the trinity would gradually become clearer over the passage of redemptive revelation).

---

8. Ibid., 152. For a sharply contrasting interpretation, see my "Doctrinal Development in Scripture and Tradition: A Reformed Assessment of the Church's Theological Task," *CTJ* 30 (1995) 401–418; republished in my *Covenant Theology in Reformed Perspective*.

As image-bearer and federal head of all humankind, the latter feature was not an afterthought: Adam was *covenantally* related to his heavenly Father and Creator, hence a "son of God" who would beget, after successful probation, others sons (and daughters). Angels and men shared this divine sonship, the former created as a host, the latter as a race. The redemptive work of the Second Adam, Jesus Christ, was requisite if there would be both reconciliation between God and fallen humanity and cosmic renewal of God's creation (with the arrival of the new heavens and new earth). Covenant and eschatology are mutually interpretive: There is a definite goal in God's purposes for all creation, summed up for the Reformed tradition in the doctrine of the glorification of God's person and works. This doctrine maintains that all that transpires is a manifestation of the glory and wisdom of our sovereign God. Election and reprobation fall within the purpose and plan of God, who has predestined whatsoever comes to pass, working all things according to his own good pleasure. The doctrine of the election of sinners *in Christ Jesus* receives extensive attention in the Pauline letters (along with the doctrines of adoption, justification, and other so-called "benefits" of the atonement or spiritual union with Christ).

The structure of biblical history is likewise covenantal through and through. The first order of creation was informed by the Covenant of Works established by God with Adam right at the outset of human history. That is to say, the Covenant of Works was not an arrangement superimposed upon a (prior) "natural" order of divine government. The notion of covenant as subsequent to the initial creation is not biblical, but speculative (resulting in a number of scholastic misformulations of scriptural revelation). At the beginning of history there is covenant and there is probation—both of these features point to the eschatological goal of creation respecting both the angelic host and the human race. What distinguishes angelic and human probation is the federal principle of representation, the righteous (or unrighteous) act of the one standing in the place of the many who are represented by the federal head. The imputation of sin or righteousness pertains only to the race of men. Hence, subsequent to the Fall, the incarnation of the Son of God would be necessary in the procurement of man's redemption. The saving work of Christ, first announced to our parents in the Garden after their transgression, introduces the second covenant, the Covenant of Grace—denoting *gospel* grace, the way of salvation by grace through saving faith. (There are only two kinds of divine grace in the Bible, both operating in the post-Fall era. They are common grace, the extension of temporal life and blessing in the world lasting until the end of the age, and saving grace, the gift of eternal life and salvation for the elect of God.) Biblical history is the record of the several covenants established by God with his people from the time of creation to the climax of covenant history, the death and resurrection of Jesus Christ, in whom was instituted the new and better covenant (new and better in comparison to the ancient Mosaic covenant). The new covenant is the final administration of the Covenant of Grace which endures until the close of world history. The essence of redemptive covenant is that God would be the God of his elect people. This is the *proper purpose* of the covenants God established in the course of redemptive history. With the coming of Christ the Covenant of Grace would be sacramentally administered by means of baptism and the observance of the Lord's Supper.

The revelation of the grand design of God's saving purpose in election in the Old Testament age would await the time of Abraham, father of all the faithful. The promise to Abraham was part of the progressive unfolding of God's redemptive purpose, announced at the beginning to our first parents after their fall into sin. The old covenant is the time of the Mosaic institution of the law with its various ordinances and rituals designed for the theocratic people of Israel. The Mosaic economy of redemption reintroduced the works-principle of inheritance (the principle that was operative in the first covenant with Adam before sin entered the scene). But as an administration of the overarching Covenant of Grace, this works-principle under Moses could not operate in the eternal, spiritual realm—only in the temporal, physical realm (namely, the typological world of Canaan, symbol of the heavenly Jerusalem). Were the law of Moses given as a means of salvation, the law would then be in competition with, and in contradiction to, the promise of the Gospel. The works-principle of inheritance would have nullified the faith-principle. Rather, the legal principle pertained exclusively and restrictively, according to divine purpose and design, to temporal life in the land of promise. Teaching concerning the Covenant of Works and the Covenant of Grace occupies a central position in the Reformed theological system; it is pivotal in the interpretation of the Bible.[9] To be sure, there was a degree of diversity in Calvinistic formulation regarding the history and theology of the divine covenants. But the main outline of covenantal history, including the meaning and significance of the divine covenants, was shared in common by all within the Reformed tradition. Old and New Testament theology (i.e., the discipline of biblical theology,

---

9. See the related doctrine of "republication," analyzed in chapter 6.

in distinction from systematic theology) weaves together the various doctrines of the Bible—such as christology, typology, and eschatology—in terms of the progressive unfolding of the Covenant of Grace in the history of redemption. The development is treated redemptive-historically, rather than "logically" or systematically. (The two methodological approaches complement one another, not conflict.)

Hermeneutics: The Science (or Art) of Interpretation

The interpretation of the Bible is a science, or more exactly, an art. Sound exegesis and theological exposition require not merely the application of valid principles and methods of interpretation, but the community of faith (namely, the Christian tradition) as a vital, confessional witness to the eternal Word revealed in the person of Jesus Christ. This living tradition spans generations of faithful saints holding forth the full counsel of God. God's own Spirit ultimately assures the genuine progress of doctrine in the life and history of the church. Each generation of confessors is a transmitter of the Christian tradition, passing along the faith from one generation to the next. Theology is a churchly activity; formal training in theology properly belongs in Christian schools of learning, not in secular academies. The modernist would have us think that confessionalism is naïve, and intolerant of truth in its diversity. We are told that truth can only be discerned in relative terms, apprehension and understanding subject to the interpreter's time and place in history and culture (broadly defined). Knowledge of the "truth," as best we might hope to attain, is temporal, not eternal—relative, not unchanging. Postmodernism, as a modification of classic liberalism, recognizes the formative role exercised by the religious community in its defining of values and beliefs; yet it assumes the relativity and changeable character of all human knowledge.

Reformed Protestantism boldly and fearlessly proclaims the truth of Scripture as the infallible, inerrant Word of God. At the heart of biblical revelation is the doctrine of the divine covenants, the engagement of a personal God with the world he has created. And at the heart of God's covenantal dealings with humankind is the sovereign election of all those chosen in Christ Jesus unto salvation. Theistic presuppositionalism is not fideistic; rather, true reason is informed by Scripture by means of the illuminating work of the Holy Spirit. Christian proclamation and apologetical defense of the one, true Gospel require witness to Christ resting upon God's special revelation. The Scripture principle of the self-attesting Christ speaking in the Scriptures stands in complete opposition to any and all supposed canons of autonomous, human rationality. The science or art of biblical interpretation is Spirit-controlled. Scripture is its own interpreter; and the Spirit of God is our true teacher.

Section Two

The Formal and Material Principles of the Protestant Reformation

Chapter Three

Revelation and Scripture
God's Covenantal Engagement

THE TERM "COVENANT" IN the Bible is both a noun and a verb. God establishes his covenant with humanity as a relationship under sanctions (blessing for obedience and curse for transgression). And divine covenant is formalized in Scripture by adoption and modification of the ancient Near Eastern suzerainty-treaty form. Utilizing this formal structure, God sovereignly enters into relationship and commitment to Israel, representative of all creation, in accordance with his own purpose and good will. Covenant-making is wholly consistent with God's nature and personhood.[1] The triune interpenetration and interaction of the persons are wholly unique and peculiar to the Godhead. By definition (that is, by the usage and meaning of the term in Scripture), "covenant" is *external* to the nature and being of God. It has been suggested by some Reformed interpreters that the relationship of the three persons within the Godhead is inherently covenantal.[2] But covenant, by biblical definition, is a relationship under sanctions.

---

1. Cornelius Van Til observes: "According to the Confession, Scripture speaks to sinners in terms of a covenant. It tells us that man was originally placed on earth under the terms of the covenant of works. It informs us further that man broke this covenant of works and that God was pleased to make a second covenant with men that they might be saved. Thus Scripture may be said to be the written expression of God's covenant relationship with man" (Stonehouse and Woolley, *The Infallible Word*, 264).

2. The most recent attempt is found in Ralph Smith, *Eternal Covenant*. In the course of argument the author, following the lead of Norman Shepherd and others, erroneously jettisons the Reformed doctrine of the Covenant of Works. See Shepherd, *The Call of Grace*. Another and very different attempt at explaining the social nature of the Trinity is

Section Two: The Formal and Material Principles

Attributing such a relationship to the triune Godhead is both inappropriate and inconceivable. The eternal being of the three persons—Father, Son, and Holy Spirit—is unique and self-subsistent. To be sure, certain analogies do exist between the intra-personal relations of the three persons and the divine-human relationship in covenant. Love as commitment conveys one important feature of the covenant bond, exemplified most familiarly in the marriage "contract." (Human covenants and contracts share similar features. There is a *contractual* element in divine covenant-making. More on this in later chapters.)

The Covenant-Making God: Divine Accommodation

The manifestation of God-in-covenant, therefore, has regard to all that is external to God's own nature and person. All that God does in his creation is by way of covenant; nothing that is done in the world is done apart from God's covenanting. It is divine *condescension* (not "grace") that characterizes God's covenantal engagement with the world he has created. Divine beneficence, however, is different from God's manifestation of (soteric) grace—what in Scripture uniquely distinguishes God's work in the redemptive era. Here again, some Reformed interpreters have mistakenly regarded God's covenant with Adam at the opening of human history as a *gracious* disposition on the part of God.[3] It is thought that the infinite God cannot relate to finite creation (including humankind) apart from an act of pure, unmitigated grace ("mercy"). According to this viewpoint, all that humanity enjoys from the good and beneficent hand of God is unearned, unmerited; all is a gift of sovereign grace. (Problems in this view are encountered when we consider the nature and necessity of the incarnation and the atoning work of Jesus the Messiah, the Son of God. Many today erroneously argue that Christ's substitutionary obedience in his work of atonement is non-meritorious, insisting that the idea of "meritorious" reward is foreign

---

found in Gruenler, *The Trinity in the Gospel of John*. Numerous other works in contemporary theology have likewise explored this theme.

3. The term "grace" has oftentimes been used in a non-redemptive (i.e., non-soteric) sense. Debate among contemporary Reformed expositors regarding the doctrine of the Covenant of Works is partly semantic, partly substantive (that is to say, theological). The words of Van Til, however, bear repeating here: "The necessity of Scripture lies in the fact that man has broken the covenant of works. He therefore needs the grace of God. There is no speech or knowledge of grace in nature. God has accordingly condescended to reveal it in Scripture" (Stonehouse and Woolley, *The Incarnate Word*, 264–65).

to the ways of God.[4]) The biblical doctrine of creaturely finitude is reflected in the familiar and essential Creator/creature distinction. The important point to be made here is that *God accommodates the revelation of his person and work to human capacity.* Calvin was particularly alert to man's utter dependence upon God; he understood the infinite distance between the Creator and the creature. That distance could only be bridged by God himself, in the person of his Son, active in the creation of the world (Col 1:15,16; Heb 1:1–3). All divine revelation is mediated through the Son (pre-incarnate and incarnate), the eternal Word. In him all things exist and have their meaning/relationship. Divine covenant is the precise means whereby God communicates his Word and will. Relationship with God is covenantal from beginning to end. This eternal bond will be consummated in the Eschaton, resulting in the glorification of the saints in the Spirit.

Hendrikus Berkhof, a leading representative of neoorthodoxy, assesses the revelatory work of God in all religions. He notes: "The thesis *all religions are based on revelation* is derived from the phenomenology of religion, where it is meant to note a fact which can be more accurately described in this way: 'all religions live by the conviction that the absolute is known through revelation.' Not only is this thesis correct, but it almost sounds like a tautology."[5] To be sure, elements of divine truth are (through general revelation) reflected in human life and thought, including religious belief and unbelief, whatever shape that may take. The critical question is whether saving truth is found in biblical religion alone, or in all religions. Berkhof forthrightly rejects the particularity of the gospel of Christ Jesus, revealed in shadow (Old Testament) and in reality (New Testament). For Berkhof the Christian gospel is *normative* of divine truth, but not *exclusive*. More exactly, it is normative for the *Christian* community of faith.

According to neoorthodoxy, there is a *hiddenness* to divine revelation which makes all human understanding elusive and tenuous. Reformed epistemology, on the other hand, maintains that our (analogical) knowledge of God and the world is authentic and certain. As finite creatures made

---

4. Such was the view of Norman Shepherd. See footnote 2 above.

5. Berkhof, *Christian Faith*, 45. Berkhof rejects the distinction between general and special revelation as misleading and inaccurate. "The contrast general-special, suggesting a kind of break between biblical revelation and what passes for revelation outside of it, is also insufficiently able to show the common background of both, or, stated differently, how the revelational event is rooted in the world of its time. The terminology is too imprecise to indicate the historical connection and growth and the dialectical relation between God's concern with the nations and his concern with Israel" (ibid., 75).

in the likeness of God, we are capable—at the finite level of ontology and epistemology—of receiving and comprehending divine truth. Human language is reflective of divine language, the speech of God declared in general and special revelation, most especially in the person of the self-attesting Christ speaking in the inscripturated Word. There is no tension or conflict between personal communication (Christ speaking in the Scriptures) and propositional statement (the doctrines of the faith set forth in Scripture and church dogma). True apprehension of the Word of God requires the effectual working of the Spirit in and with the Word. In an effort to escape the dilemma which neorthodoxy has created for itself, this school of interpretation has taken recourse to biblical narrative (story-telling) as the means of articulating the Christian faith. Christianity is essentially the record of God's action in history; it is not dogma, so we are told.

The accommodation of God's revelation to human capacity necessitates the theological distinction between truth as it is in God himself (he being the *archetype*) and truth as it is made known to the sons of God through general and special revelation (theology as the *ectype*). This also points to the necessity of divine condescension in all God's external works, including his self-revelation. The heavens declare the glory of God; heaven and earth, the spiritual and physical realms, reflect the wisdom, power, and glory of God. These two creaturely kingdoms are ectypal manifestations of the eternal Spirit-Presence of God who upholds all things by his powerful, sovereign hand. God is both transcendent and immanent, the One who inspires awe, wonder, and praise for his vast and manifold creation.[6]

---

6. Van Til writes: "God's revelation in nature, together with God's revelation in Scripture, form God's one grand scheme of covenant revelation of himself to man. The two forms of revelation must therefore be seen as presupposing and supplementing one another. They are aspects of one general philosophy of history" (Stonehouse and Woolley, *The Incarnate Word*, 267). Hendrikus Berkhof views the assemblage of sacred writings as pure historical circumstance, rather than special, divine providence. He explains: "Eventually these documents were collected into larger units. And finally this process came to an end because a consensus was reached concerning the scope and the limits of the body of documents that could be regarded as the written fixation of the event of revelation" (*Christian Faith*, 79). With the advent of the science of historical criticism "we may have quite different ideas about the 'authenticity' of some of the documents than those who long ago included them in the canon. However, what we today can no longer accept as authoritative fixation, we can often appreciate as an example of interpretive transmission. The canon which we now have contains very varied and often contradictory reactions to the revelational process. So this canon reminds us that the revelation is not a system or an ideology, but an encounter of the living God with living people in history. The unity of Scripture does not lie in itself but in the oneness of the God who remains the same in

Natural and Supernatural Revelation

Human comprehension of the self and the world is dependent upon both general and special revelation, the latter being the supernatural communication to humankind by way of theophany. At the outset, Adam and Eve were recipients of God's spoken word, special revelation emanating from the divine Council, the throne-room of God in the heavenly abode, humankind's ultimate residence. The divine presence is most frequently portrayed throughout Scripture (Old and New Testaments) as the Glory-Spirit in exceedingly rich and complex ways. The Spirit-theophany, what is implicitly trinitarian, is first introduced to us in the Mosaic account of creation in Genesis 1:2. (Here the triunity of God is manifested in the presence of the angelic hosts, which together with the triune God comprise the divine Council.) The Spirit communicates the Word of the Father in and though the Son, who is the Word eternal. All creation is brought into being by the working of the three persons of the Godhead.

Unlike Protestantism, Roman Catholicism posits three sources of revelation—nature, Scripture, and church tradition (the last includes the doctrine of papal infallibility). The teaching office of the Roman church is thought to have equal weight with Scripture in the interpretation of natural and special revelation. Further, Roman Catholicism insists that human reason, unaided by supernatural grace (that is, the Spirit of regeneration and illumination), is capable of discerning the truths of God revealed in nature, even to the extent of articulating a "natural theology," in distinction from (though complementary to) a theology of the Word, as it understands it.

Protestantism, on the other hand, maintains that the finite creature, even in his unfallen state, cannot interpret or understand natural revelation apart from special revelation. Natural and supernatural revelation are mutually interpretive; both are necessary. And since the Fall, the finite creature is entirely dependent upon the regenerating work of the Spirit of God for true knowledge. The work of God the Spirit has epistemological as well as soteriological ramifications. Succinctly put, Scripture being the infallible Word of God is the sole rule of faith and practice. It is not a matter of Scripture *and* church tradition.[7]

---

the continually changing encounters" (ibid., 80).

7. Louis Berkhof insightfully remarks: "Without revelation man would never have been able to acquire any knowledge of God. And even after God has revealed Himself objectively, it is not human reason that discovers God, but it is God who discloses Himself to the eye of faith. However, by the application of sanctified human reason to the study

Neoorthodoxy,[8] the school of thought that became dominant in twentieth-century theology and continues to exercise its influence, contends that human apprehension of the Word of God through the exercise of faith is an *Event* or an *Encounter* with the unseen. The essence of Christianity is thought to be a religious encounter, an experience that cannot be reduced to a set of doctrinal "propositions" descriptive of God in his relationship to the created order. Historic Protestantism rejects this modern doctrine as a repudiation of the self-attesting, authoritative Word of God. God's Word cannot be reduced to an existential, personal human-divine Encounter. The Reformed tradition, following the clear and persuasive teaching of Calvin, has properly recognized the necessity of the inscripturated Word as the sole norm for Christian doctrine and life, and the Spirit as our true, ultimate interpreter. (Thus Calvin joined together Word and Spirit as interdependent for the apprehension of truth.)

The Glory-Spirit as Divine Paradigm

Genuine knowledge of God is imparted by the Spirit, the creator-God who sustains, illumines, and governs all creation. The mirroring of the Glory of God is realized by way of the theophanic Spirit who breathes out light, life, and immortality. The Glory-Spirit has a formative role in general and special revelation, in nature and in Scripture. He is the divine Paradigm, the heavenly archetype of truth and life eternal. Creation, original and renewed in Christ, is the theater of God's Glory manifested in the Spirit. The Spirit first breathed life into Adam, forming him in the image and likeness of God. Adam was created a "natural body." Subsequent to the Fall, the eschatological Spirit of Christ transforms the body of believers into a "spiritual

---

of God's Word man can, under the guidance of the Holy Spirit, gain an ever-increasing knowledge of God" (*Systematic Theology*, 34).

8. Given the growing impact neoorthodoxy is having at present, mastery of its theology is especially critical in the study of contemporary evangelical-Reformed interpretation. Various teachings of this school of interpretation continue to gain ground in once-conservative, confessional theology to a very alarming degree. We are using the term "neoorthodox" in a somewhat elastic manner to cover a wide spectrum of modern interpretation, all of which share some of the same theological preconceptions, ideas that are alien to biblical, Reformed theology (in its historic definition and exposition). Attempts to recast contemporary Reformed theology in a way that will free itself from "stodgy" confessionalism (of the scholastic orthodox variety!) and open up new avenues of interpretation and dialogue can be found in John Frame's multiperspectivalism and John Franke's revisionist theology. (See chapter two.)

organism" (the church, the Body of Christ). Spiritual renewal comes as the result of the redemptive work of Christ, who through his atonement and glorification became life-giving Spirit (1 Cor 15:44, 45).

In his wise providence, the covenant Lord was pleased to inscripturate, i.e., set down in writing his revelation to Israel, the ancient, theocratic people of God. The Lord God raised up Moses as mediator of the old covenant, the covenant ratified by Israel in the wilderness of Sinai. Here was redemptive re-creation, the resumption of the original purpose of God in creation in the fallen world torn and ravaged by sin and its consequences. The initial announcement of the *protevangelium* (the promise of the good news of the Gospel) was declared to our first parents prior to their expulsion from the Garden of Eden. The prospect of (re)entrance into Eden (typological Canaan) had become a redemptive-eschatological hope to be realized by the recreating Spirit of God remaking and refashioning the created order into the everlasting Temple of God, the Body of Christ, having its final dwelling-place in the new heavens and earth (Revelation 21 and 22).⁹ Before and after the Fall, the Edenic garden symbolizes God's eternal

---

9. There is an intimate connection between the two Testaments, wherein the former is the precursor to the latter. Here again the divine covenants provide the structural or "architectural" ground for the historical account of redemptive revelation. Meredith G. Kline observes: "For the historical relationship sustained by the new covenant to the old covenant and the place occupied by the New Testament as the divine documentation of the new covenant compel us to understand the New Testament as a resumption of that documentary mode of covenant administration represented by the Old Testament" (*The Structure of Biblical Authority*, 68).

Hendrikus Berkhof presupposes that the writing of the Old and New Testament scriptures was simply part and parcel of human (religious) experience. "Eventually—for it is only natural that there is first a period of oral tradition. But that can only be temporary. The written fixation commonly happens when the distance between the events and the present can no longer be bridged by ear-and eyewitnesses, and when the twofold danger of oral tradition, namely abridgment and trimming, and elaboration and embellishment, becomes too great" (*Christian Faith*, 78). Contrary to neoorthodox teaching, the canon(s) of Scripture is more than the product of historical circumstance. It is the inspired, written revelation of God, unified in all its teachings (hence, devoid of contradictory statement). Compare the *Westminster Confession of Faith*, chapter 1. The Protestant-Reformed doctrine of Scripture calls into question contemporary methods of redaction and literary criticism (including the interpretation known as *midrash*). Modern biblical criticism posits a creative, developmental view of doctrine among the conveyers of the faith-tradition, wherein historical retelling, both as modification and as embellishment, is taken as normative. Midrashic interpretation differs significantly from typological (or christological) interpretation of the Old Testament. According to the latter, history (i.e., his story) is understood to be in all details, and in its fullest extent, foreordained, Old Testament history being preparatory to the coming of the Messiah,

sabbath-rest, into which rest the redeemed people of God will enter in consummate glory at the end of the age.

Miraculously and memorably on the cloud-shrouded mountain, the first portion of the inscripturated Word, the Decalogue, was crafted by the very finger of God. These Ten Commandments, spread across two sides of a stone tablet, the second tablet being a duplicate of the first (a familiar legal custom in the ancient near eastern world), were a summary of God's law to theocratic Israel, the law that would be fully explicated in the five books of Moses, the Pentateuch. Human writing was a recent innovation, first appearing in Sumer and rapidly developing elsewhere in the ancient Mediterranean world. (Obviously, Egyptian hieroglyphics did not facilitate easy, nor precise [clear], communication. The languages of Sumerian, Akkadian, and Ugaritic all contributed to the rise and development of the language of the ancient Jewish people, Hebrew and Aramaic.) We might say that in the "fullness of (OT) times" God raised up Moses to lead and instruct the Hebrew people, those chosen to be God's elect nation. (Note here, however, that national election is different from personal, decretive election to salvation.) Theocratic Israel, servant of the Lord, would prepare the way for Israel's Messiah, God's true Servant, faithful keeper of the covenant under Moses. The old economy of redemption is redolent with christological and typological signification. (The *modified* Covenant of Works first manifest at creation served in the Mosaic order of theocratic life as an overlay to the Covenant of Grace, which administered the redemptive blessings to the elect, and to them only.)

At the signal moment of the birth of Israel as a theocratic nation, whose constitution was the Book of the Covenant (to be expanded in the giving of the second law, the Book of Deuteronomy, appropriately called the "Treaty of the Great King"),[10] all the salient features of the ancient suzerainty-treaties are present: preamble and historical prologue, stipulations and sanctions, dynastic disposition. Out of pure, sovereign, unmerited grace the Lord God covenants with his elect people, promising a kingdom which would endure forever. (Earthly Palestine was only typological of the eternal inheritance. Life in Canaan was only temporary in duration, until Christ should come and establish the new and better covenant.) The God of Israel is the God of redemptive covenant. Israel's deliverance from the

---

God's anointed One. Midrash, broadly speaking, is the church's *creative* retelling and reapplication of ancient, sacred texts in new cultural and historical settings.

10. See Kline, *Treaty of the Great King*.

power of dominion under Egypt—the embodiment of the forces of evil and antichrist—brings temporal (typological) victory, as well as the assurance of God's protecting arm for the wilderness journey which lay ahead of the Israelites. The blueprint for Israel's (national) life in Canaan, the land of promise, is the law of Moses, to which nothing was to be added or subtracted. The covenant-word of the Suzerain is inviolate, requiring complete, total allegiance from his vassal people. Disobedience would bring upon Israel the deserved wrath and displeasure of God (exemplified in the days of Babylonian captivity, anticipatory of the abrogation of the Mosaic economy of redemption and the final destruction of the earthy temple in Jerusalem).

The Witness of Scripture as Word of God

The Word of divine revelation summons Israel to walk in the way of repentance and faith. Protestant dogmatics has given careful and exhaustive attention to the nature and attributes of Scripture as the authoritative, written revelation of God. Theologians of the sixteenth-and seventeenth-century Reformation affirmed the necessity of Scripture as the written source of supernatural revelation (made necessary by virtue of God's decree and special superintendence of the church from the time of Moses onwards until the end of the age[11]). The sufficiency of Scripture has regard to the salvation of sinners and instruction in the things of God. The efficacy of Scripture relates to the certainty that God's Word will accomplish God's purpose in the edification and building of the spiritual Temple, the New Man in Christ Jesus. Other attributes of Scripture include the perfection (and finality) of Scripture as special revelation (hence, the close of the canons of Scripture, old and new) and the perspicuity/clarity of Scripture in its record of redemptive history, and the elucidation of doctrinal and ethical teaching for the people of God.[12] The Bible conveys the authority of God himself, the author and preserver of his infallible Word.

---

11. Prior to this time, God was pleased to convey his (unwritten) special revelation among the covenant people by means of oral tradition. Inscripturation of special revelation has helped deter corruption and misrepresentation of God's self-communication in the transmission of true religion among succeeding generations.

12. No attribute of Scripture has been more widely (and subtly) undermined in recent Reformed theology and hermeneutics than that relating to Scripture's perspicuity. Today, the problem is said to lie in the interpretation of Scripture itself; and the problem, we are told, is inherent in the tenuous nature of the Christian theology. Doctrinal formulation is relegated to one's place in history and culture. We are told that we can only arrive at an

Section Two: The Formal and Material Principles

Later evangelical Protestant theology coined the term "inerrancy" in its doctrine of Scripture to further explicate the attribute of divine perfection in God's written revelation. Simply stated, Scripture is free from error. What is set forth in the pages of the Bible, rightly interpreted, does not misstate or misrepresent truth revealed by God.[13] The same God who inspired the human authors as instruments in the process of the inscripturation of the Word also illumines the minds of faithful believers who eagerly receive the sacred writings with joy and devotion. The Spirit's work in inspiration and superintendence ensures the purity and the inerrancy of the written revelation throughout the ages.

Perhaps the most important, single attribute of Scripture is divine inspiration. It is not uncommon for one for conclude, upon listening to a stirring performance of George Frederick Handel's *Messiah*, that the composer was "inspired" by God. Yet, the use of this term in this context is not only inappropriate, it is inaccurate. Just as the Spirit breathed life into Adam at his creation in the image of God, so too the Spirit is universally at work in the world sustaining, governing, and bringing all things that come to pass. However, the Spirit's work in inspiring human authors in the writing of sacred scripture was unique. This work of the Spirit guaranteed the accurate, infallible and inerrant recording of God's special revelation (2 Tim 3:16 and 2 Pet 1:20–21). The mystery of divine and human factors in the process of inscripturation is an article of Christian faith receiving and

---

approximate understanding of what the Bible teaches.

13. E. J. Young explains in "The Authority of the Old Testament" (Stonehouse and Woolley, eds., *The Infallible Word,* 74): "[T]hat which determines the canonicity of any book is the book's inspiration. A book which is inspired by God therefore, is *ipso facto* canonical." Meredith G. Kline relates biblical canonicity specifically to redemptive covenant. "Biblical canonicity shows itself from its inception to be of the lineage of covenantal canonicity" (*The Structure of Biblical Authority,* 37). The writings of Scripture, comprising Old and New Testament canons, are properly viewed as the official documents of the covenant(s) transacted between God and his people over the course of two different, yet at the same time similar, economies of redemption. Unlike the former, the New Testament canon was completed in a relatively short period of time, covering only the period of the inauguration of the new covenant (approximately a fifty-year span). The Old Testament canon regulated ancient, theocratic Israel in a comparatively longer period of preparation and anticipation for the coming of the Messiah and for the establishment of the new and better covenant (what yielded the New Testament canon of the Christian church.) See Chapter Four.

The biblical canons of Old and New Testaments were recognized by the early Christians as together comprising the church's Scriptures. It was the Spirit of God who enabled the church to receive these books—and only these books—as the inscripturated Word. Consult further, the *Westminster Confession of Faith*, chapter one.

resting upon the Word of God written by men, yet divinely inspired and free from all error.[14]

Again, comparison with the teaching of neoorthodoxy (or Barthianism) is helpful at this point. With respect to the doctrine of Scripture, neoorthodox interpreters maintain that Scripture is not the Word of God in some literalistic (formalistic or "abstract") sense. Rather, according to this school of thought, Scripture *becomes* the Word of God in the divine-human Encounter. Scripture is merely *witness* to the revelatory Event. Christian theology, in turn, is the church's reflection on the meaning and relevance of Christian faith as a further witness to the Word revealed in the church's sacred text, the Bible. In both the Barthian and existential schools theology, in the final analysis, is *application* (human appropriation).

The doctrine of Scripture has immediate ties to churchly interpretation, exegetical and theological. Hermeneutical methodology, the science or practice of biblical interpretation, is derived from the Bible, not something imposed upon it. Scripture and theology (church dogmatics) are inextricably related to one another. We were first introduced to the science of hermeneutics in Chapter Two, dealing with theological prolegomena (or first-principles). Here we note that the scopus or center of Scripture is Jesus Christ, the incarnate Word of God, the Word made flesh for the sake of the redemption of those once alienated from God, lying under his just wrath and condemnation (see Lk 24:13–49). Scripture is self-authenticating: As the living, active Word of God, Scripture speaks on the authority of Christ who reveals the Father to us. All three persons of the Trinity have a distinctive role in bringing the written Word into being and in opening the minds of fallen sinners to receive that Word as divine truth. In terms of

---

14. Remember here that the church's reception of the canons of Scripture, Old and New Testaments, was/is not based on sacred writing meeting a list of criteria (outside Scripture) as a means of authenticating genuine canonicity (what amounts to the implementation of a human-devised standard separate from the Word of God). Scripture is uniquely authoritative and self-authenticating. The Protestant-Reformed teaching concerning the canons of Scripture requires the cessation of ongoing revelation in the life of the church subsequent to the close of the apostolic age. With the completion of the twofold canon there is no further special revelation until the second appearance of Christ at the end of the age. Among the features often listed as marks of canonicity are factuality, coherence, and unity of doctrine. The problem is that human reason is incapable of making this determination. Who among us—down the corridors of church history—can ultimately say that this book, and not that book, belongs to the canon of Scripture? It is only by means of the witness of the Spirit among the community of the faithful, the outworking of divine providence. See again, the *Westminster Confession of Faith*, chapters one and five.

their distinctive work in the economy of redemption, the Father reveals, the Son reconciles, the Spirit regenerates. It was the Protestant reformer John Calvin who gave special emphasis to the internal witness of the Spirit. He underscored the convicting and convincing testimony of the Spirit in and with the Word of Christ in the hearts and minds of true believers.[15]

---

15. John Murray observes: "the internal testimony does not convey to us new truth content. The whole truth content that comes within the scope of the internal testimony is contained in the Scripture" (Stonehouse and Woolley, *The Infallible Word*, 52). On the matter of divine authority borne in the written Word, contrast the opinion of H. Berkhof: "It is doubtful whether the term 'authority' is quite relevant in reference to the encounter with God in Christ. Paul describes what happens in this encounter in the words: 'it is the Spirit himself bearing witness with our spirit that we are children of God' (Rom 8:16). And the life based on this he describes as a life of freedom and confidence. Can one justly apply to this life the term 'authority' with its correlates of obedience and subjection" (*Christian Faith*, 86)? Redefining the concept, he states that "if the relationship of Scripture and revelation is indirect, then the authority of Scripture is also of an indirect character. Concretely this means: first, with an authoritative voice Scripture refers us to the revelation; next, on the authority of what we have understood of the revelation we evaluate the testimonies of Scripture, and so there arises an interaction between them. The concept of the 'authority of Scripture' is part of this process and is qualified by it. One who tries to use it apart form that context fails to recognize the indirect relationship between revelation and Scripture and cannot, or only with difficulty, do justice to the humanness, the historicity, and the variety in the Scriptural testimonies" (ibid., 87).

Chapter Four

God and Humanity
Eden Lost and Regained

IN THE BEGINNING THE eternal, self-existing God created time and space. The first eleven chapters of Genesis record the *primeval history of the world*, history that was infallibly and inerrantly conveyed to Moses through the supernatural illumination and inspiration of the Holy Spirit. This history could partly be gleaned from oral tradition, partly from written sources then available in the ancient Near East—for example, the Babylonian flood stories and other (mythological) accounts of creation and the "world that then was" (2 Pet 2:5; 3:5–7). Genesis history, however, is altogether different from myth or saga. The biblical record is accurate in its historical veracity—in its account(s) of the creation of the world, the fall of our first parents into sin, the spiritual conflict with the Serpent (the Devil), the great flood in the days of Noah, and other history leading up to the call of Abraham, father of all the faithful. At the same time, however, Moses recounted this history in a manner that defies the method and standards of modern scientific historiography (as though they should govern our reading and interpretation of the biblical authors!). Furthermore, Moses did display his superb literary craft in the writing of the Pentateuch, a gift of God to his servant the prophet. Any later, minor editorial work on the Pentateuch (such as the record of Moses' death) was likewise governed by the Holy Spirit in the production of the autographs. Similarly, the Spirit preserved the inscripturated Word in its transmission down through the ages.[1]

---

1. Redaction criticism posits the widespread practice of retelling or reinterpreting sacred history and doctrine throughout the course of the transmission of Scripture, prior

SECTION TWO: THE FORMAL AND MATERIAL PRINCIPLES

The Revelation of the God of Glory

Of paramount interest in the Book of Genesis is the record of the history leading up to the formation and constitution of Israel as the chosen, theocratic people of God, the subject of Exodus and the remaining books of the Pentateuch. Central to this historical account is the progressive unfolding of the series of divine covenants established by God with his people, beginning in the Garden of Eden with what is called the Covenant of Works and resuming with the second covenant, the Covenant of Grace extending from the Fall to the Consummation. The composition of the Pentateuch follows the pattern of ancient Near Eastern treaty documents in very unique and creative ways. The apt description of Genesis as "Kingdom Prologue" captures both the purpose and the content of this opening book in the Pentateuch.[2]

God discloses his name to Moses: He is *Yahweh,* covenant Lord of Israel. He is the creator of the world and Israel's redeemer, the One who manifests himself by way of *Glory-theophany.* This visible manifestation of God—for the benefit of his creatures—is normative in the unfolding revelation of God in covenant with his people in both the old and new economies of redemption. The Glory-Counsel, what is descriptive of this divine theophany or appearance of God, is the deliberative session of God the Father surrounded by his myriad angels, those who had successfully passed probation in the time prior to man's appearance in the Garden. Standing at the right hand of the Father is God the Son, the eternal Word of God, in whom all things were made.

Yahweh, Israel's God, the true and only God, the God of all the nations, freely creates the cosmos as a reflection of his own glory and splendor. This same glory is manifested on various levels in the created order, macrocosmic and microcosmic (for example, in the earthly tabernacle and temple). God was not obliged to create the universe; he was not in need of the company of angels and humankind. Having determined to create all things in heaven and on earth for his own glory, God *condescended* to reveal himself in covenant with all creation. All verbal revelation, oracular and inscripturated, is anthropomorphic. That is to say, God communicates his Word and will to finite creatures who have been given the capacity to

---

to the formation (and adoption) of the Jewish and Christian canons. Allegedly, redactionary activity was heightened in the time of Israel's exile from Palestine and in the time of the early Christian communities, when the biblical writers set about to render (competing) accounts of the history and teachings of Jesus and his disciples.

2. Meredith G. Kline, *Kingdom Prologue.*

receive and understand God's revelation. Knowledge of the truth and will of God is *truly known* by man as receptor; but that truth which man is given to know is *analogical* to God's self-knowledge. There is a fundamental difference between the knowledge which God possesses as infinite and eternal in his being and the knowledge that man possesses as finite and derivative. Divine ontology informs human epistemology: Man cannot know—not now and not in the world to come—God's thoughts precisely as God knows them, nor in the same manner. This follows from the basic Creator/creature distinction explicitly taught in Scripture, and premised in all of its pages.

Theology proper begins with a consideration of God as he is in himself (the doctrine of divine aseity). God is self-existent and self-contained. He exists as the triune personality—Father, Son, and Holy Spirit. The personhood of God is one and three, a mystery transcending finite, human comprehension. The doctrine of the Trinity is accepted, not because it passes the test of human reasonableness (abstract rationality), but because God has so revealed himself. Divine revelation is inherently trinitarian and covenantal. There is a similarity between God's triune personality and covenantal engagement with his creation. Covenantal relationship is inherently personal; it is the relationship between persons, divine and human. By extension, God's relationship with the cosmos is likewise covenantal, a relationship based upon divine promise and commitment—for the sake of humanity created in his image and likeness. God pledges to uphold the work of his hands both in creation and in recreation, a commitment summoning the intra-trinitarian, intra-personal engagement of the Father, the Son, and the Spirit.

Some speak of the Godhead as a "social Trinity," a community of persons manifesting truth and love (*because* God is truth and love). Care must be taken, however, to safeguard the unique relationship and communication among the three persons. Here too there is a qualitative distinction between the social Trinity and human society, whether viewed as the marriage of a man and a woman, a socio-political compact, or as the Body of Christ, the church. One distinction is the fact that God's covenantal commitment to the world and to humanity is *ab-extra*, that is, outside of himself. *Covenant belongs to the created order of things*. There is no covenantal transaction or pledge assumed by the three persons of the Godhead in its self-existence and self-determination. There is no "meeting of the minds" determining how they exist (that is, with regard to the constitution of the divine being) and how they act (that is, fellowship and communion/relationship with angelic and human creation, and all things *ab-intra*). The ontological character of God is wholly unique and self-contained; finite creatures cannot probe into the being and mind of God *as it exists and is known to God himself.* We have only analogies between human (and human and divine) relationships indicating similarities regarding the intra-trinitarian, intra-personal relationship(s) within the Godhead. What we can confidently assert from special revelation is this: Covenant belongs to what is *ab-extra*, to what lies outside of God in his unique, singular existence (the aseity of God, the One-in-Three). Covenant involves divine condescension; and the redemption of fallen humanity necessitates the incarnation of the second person of the Trinity. The incarnation was decreed by God as the singular means of achieving reconciliation, atonement for sin, and the consummation of the Kingdom of God among men and angels. Redemption is the covenantal pledge of God-in-Christ, empowered by the Spirit who gives life, both temporal and eternal.

Creation by Divine Fiat

Prior to time and space, *God is*. This divine existence transcends time and space, so that the everlasting God is the God who is, and was, and is to come—without separation and without diminution, ever present, all-powerful, and all-knowing. Man the creature cannot (fully and exhaustively) comprehend divine existence; our being and consciousness are derivative, bound to time and space, both now and in the world to come, eternal though it shall be in the final state. According to the secondary order of things created, the eternality of the consummate Kingdom of God, including the (prior) predestinating and electing purpose of God in eternity past, is similar though distinct from God's unique eternality. If the eternal predestination of all things that would come to pass in time were to partake of God's own eternality, creation and redemption would then have had to occur. But Scripture clearly teaches that creation and redemption were a free act of God's goodness and (saving) grace, in that historical sequence.[3] We apprehend our existence and place in

---

3. Goodness characterizes the creative handiwork of God. Note the recurring affirmation in the Genesis account of creation ("and it was good"), an affirmation of God's own approbation and delight in his works. Grace characterizes the recreative handiwork of God. Grace not only contemplates human demerit (both Adam's original transgression imputed to all humanity and all other human offenses resulting from a depraved nature), it also brings to realization the completed fulfillment of the law of God in the person and work of God's own Son, the only Savior of men. Redemption includes both the forgiveness of sins (satisfied by the passive obedience of Christ) and the reward of life everlasting (secured by the active obedience of Christ). Justification by faith alone has

the world God has created in complete dependence upon the existence, the presence, and the prerogative of God who governs and sustains all things according to the purpose of his sovereign will.

According to the opening verse of the Bible, the invisible and visible world was created out of nothing, simply by the word of God's mouth, the *logos,* the eternal Word that was manifested in the beginning of all things (compare John 1, Col 1:13-29, and Heb 1:1-3). Genesis One also tells us that God brought all things into existence, each created "after its own kind" (compare 1 Cor 15:39-41). Modern, antitheistic evolutionary theory posits the eternality of matter in the form of energy; at some moment in the distant past the interaction of energetic forces is thought to have ignited a series of cataclismic events leading up to the formation of the cosmos as we now know it, including the birth and formation of the small habitat we call Earth. Humanity is viewed as the culmination of an exceedingly long period of evolutionary development that still in process. (From this theory comes the modern doctrine of "process theology," which teaches that "god" is part of the cosmos—part of one, universal Being—and is likewise in process of change and development.[4]) To the contrary, Scripture teaches that God is distinct from his creation. The cosmos, visible and invisible, is brought into existence by the direct fiat of God, not by evolutionary process and development, whether random or by "Intelligent Design." According to the Bible, God's creative work is distinct from his providential sustenance and governance of all things he has created. In "the space of six days" God created all things. The time of creation has come to a close: God has now rested from his creative activity.[5] The biblical doctrine of the Sabbath points to the goal of the consummate realization of God's purpose in creation, namely, the arrival of the eternal Kingdom of God—that supernal kingdom anticipated in different ways in the redemptive epoch, both in the formation and constitution of Israel as a (typological) kingdom of priests and kings and in the (spiritual) semi-eschatological formation of the pentecostal church of the new covenant.

---

been labeled as the *material principle* of the Protestant Reformation, the inscripturated Word of God as the *formal principle.*

4. Compare here the doctrine of open theism held by modern-day "evangelicals." Consult John Piper, Justin Taylor, and Paul Kjoss Helseth, eds., *Beyond the Bounds: Open Theism and the Undermining of Biblical Christianity.*

5. Debates over the meaning of the expression "in the space of six day" in the Westminster Confession of Faith is very contentious among conservative Reformed expositors. See *The Genesis Debate: Three views on the days of creation,* ed. David. G. Hagopian.

Section Two: The Formal and Material Principles

Modernist evolutionary theology not only rejects the biblical doctrine of creation, it also denies the historicity of Adam and Eve as our first parents, and it denies the federal, representative headship of the first Adam. Theistic evolution likewise falters in its ability to reconcile modern evolutionary theory with biblical revelation. What must be said here is that modern scientific *theory* is all-too-frequently taken as established fact by contemporary biblical interpreters. The critical test, however, is whether or not Scripture has priority over the natural sciences. The reconciliation between science and the Bible can only come about as human interpretation is founded and conducted upon the explicit (and true) revelation of God in the inscripturated Word. General and special revelation, rightly interpreted, complement one another. There is no ultimate conflict between science and true religion.[6]

Earth, humankind's habitat, in its early formation by divine fiat was yet unformed. It had not yet become suitable for human habitation. Final preparation of earth prior to the creation of Adam from the dust of the ground—and Eve from his rib—was the selection of Eden as the meeting place between God and man, the earthly sanctuary, holy ground. This site is set apart as holy unto God, a place of special meeting. The geo-political empire that Adam was commissioned to build (what is implicit in the so-called "cultural mandate" given in Gen 1:26–31) would have been constituted a *theocracy*. That earthly empire, without the devastating effects of the Fall, would have manifested God's rule and reign over all creation; it would have manifested itself as the (pre-consummate) Kingdom of God. The spread of God's rule and man's viceregency would have extended from Eden to every corner of the world, to the farthest reaches of the universe. The earth and the heavens above would have radiated the glory of God in all its perfection and beauty, without spot or blemish. Sin altered the picture, and ruptured the relationship between God and our first parents, bringing humankind under the power of death and corruption, a return to dust and ashes (see Rom 8:18–23, for a return of man's dominion over the created order on the final day of redemption).

---

6. Study in the natural sciences is circumscribed by the limitations of human epistemology, more particularly, by the nature of human finitude. God asked Job: "Where were you, o man, when I created the heavens and earth?" See R. Hooykaas, *Religion and the Rise of Modern Science*.

Probation and Image-Bearing

The setting for the contest between Adam and the serpent at the opening of human history requires us to consider the creation and probation of the angelic host. Unlike humankind, which was created as a race of peoples, the angels were created as a host, each angel standing on the integrity of his own act of obedience or disobedience. Lucifer, the prince of the angelic host, confronted God with his evil design to claim supremacy and autonomy. How evil gripped the heart of Lucifer remains a mystery in Scripture and in natural revelation. (Likewise, Adam's transgression remains an inexplicable mystery. How could Adam—created in true knowledge, righteousness, and holiness—have desired to disobey God, the giver of life and of every good gift? Certainly, the serpent deceived and deluded our first parents, but ultimately, it was the willful, sin-ridden desire of Adam to transgress God's commandment.) The perversion of God's purpose and design for creation is revealed in the human heart (by natural revelation) and by creation itself, which has turned its anger and wrath upon humankind by means of natural catastrophe, disease, and death. In a sinless world, humankind would have been protected and nurtured by the beneficent goodness of God against the powers of nature—rising flood-waters, volcanic eruptions, fire, wind, and storm (to name only a few).

Lucifer's confrontation with the Lord of Glory placed the entire angelic host on trial, a trial sovereignly decreed and purposed by God as requisite for the acclamation and testimony of God's name and lordship. Probation is the divinely-ordained means to higher perfection and glory for all intelligent creation, beginning with the angelic host, those creatures who were likewise constituted "sons of God." The angels were created perfect in righteousness, holiness, and true knowledge, subject to the Father's probation. Growth in perfection demands testing/trial demanding total obedience, what was also the case with respect to God's own Son incarnate (see Heb 2:9–18; 4:15 and 16; 5:8 and 9). The conclusion of this first trial in heaven resulted in the division between good and evil angels. Those confirmed in righteousness are privileged to serve as ministering angels on behalf of the world of humanity (before and after Adam's fall into sin). The serve as ministers of the Divine Counsel, of which they are part.

The First and Second Adams were made/placed a little lower than the angels now confirmed in righteousness. Successful completion of probation would have elevated Adam (=humanity) above the angels. Happily, what was lost by the First Adam, was gained by the Second. That is the message of the gospel, first announced to our parents in the Garden after the Fall (Gen 3:15, what is called the protevangelium). But the final reward of Christ's redemptive work would necessarily await the consummation of history. The expansion of the human race requires an extended period of time to accommodate the natural propagation of the race and the historical differentiation between the elect and the reprobate. The formation of the elect people of God would be a wholly supernatural work of God's grace and mercy, from start to finish.

As image-bearer, humanity was commissioned to serve God as priest and king, by consecrating all to the glory of God and by exercising dominion as God's viceregents over all creation. The unique prophetic office arises as the result of sin's entrance into the human race, and it consists in the universal call to repentance and obedience (the obedience of saving, justifying faith), as in the days of Noah before the Day of Judgment in the world that then was—what was an anticipation of the great and final Day of the Lord at the close of human history. The same twofold office of priest and king is conveyed to the sons of Adam over the course of the propagation of the human race and the expansion of humanity's rule over the earth. Sin, however, results in the bifurcation of the twofold office of priest and king in terms of the introduction of "common grace" into the fallen world. In order to open the field of development for the race of men (as well as to provide for the ingathering of the nations through the mission and witness of the church in the world), God graciously withholds judgment until the end of the history. The godly and the ungodly labor side by side in the common realm of human endeavor, the cultivation of earth's resources and the enhancement of human life in various societies and cultures. The true, spiritual sons of Adam alone are enabled to serve God as priests, ministering to God's praise and glory in all areas of human endeavor, sacred and secular (holy and common). There is from the beginning the universal priesthood of all believers, although the full ramifications of this spiritual office—and empowerment from the resurrected Christ on high—must await the Day of Pentecost, and the outpouring of the Spirit of Christ in the semi-eschatological age of the church.

The Spirit of God, which brooded over the chaotic waters at the beginning of earth's history, is the same Spirit which forms the new people of God out of the chaotic waters of sin's depredation. And this Spirit is the substance of the divine Glory-Counsel (all the while acknowledging the Trinitarian character of this divine counsel). Seated about the throne of

God and Humanity

God are the myriads of angels ministering at God's behest. Throughout the course of redemptive history as recorded in the pages of Scripture we read of the intersection of heaven and earth, the place of God's judicial encounter with the sons of men.[7] The God of judgment, the Glory-Spirit, makes his presence known and visible by means of *theophany*. Many of the psalms reflect upon this fearful and awesome appearance of God in the midst of Israel and the nations. It is the setting for the prophetic call of Moses, Samuel, Isaiah, and all the other prophets, former and latter-day. Exile from the land of promise in the days of Babylonian captivity marks the great (typological) Day of judgment under the old economy of redemption. Theophany is equally pervasive and transforming in the establishment of the new covenant in Christ Jesus.

Theocracy Once and Again

Eden was the site of the first theocracy on earth. Here there is no distinction between what is holy and what is common in the affairs of humankind. All human endeavor fell under the (direct and immediate) rule of God. The original theocratic institution, however, came to an abrupt halt with the transgression of our first parents. The representative act of disobedience made necessary the expulsion of Adam and Eve from the Garden of Eden, now guarded and protected by the ministering angels with sword and fire. (This judgment of God was requisite, even though Adam and Eve had become the recipients of God's mercy and grace in Christ—ultimate victors over the sin, death, and the Devil). God's marvelous, redemptive provision would be manifested over time, from seed-form to full-flower. This is what accounts for the division in the Bible between two Testaments, the former preparatory for the latter testament/covenant made with Christ's own blood.

The period from the Fall to the call of Abraham is characterized by the universal summons to repentance and faith in the God who reigns over all peoples in sovereign power and righteous judgment. Like the age of the new covenant church (the New Testament era), this opening period in redemptive history is, for the spiritual seed of Adam, the age of "grace," not "law." *Here there is no reckoning of transgression, for all believers have been forgiven and cleansed by the shed-blood of Jesus Christ, who was yet to enter the world*

---

7. The Apostle Peter locates the Noahic flood in "the world that once was" (2 Pet 3:6); we live in the world that now is. This demarcation sets apart the pre-and post-diluvian covenants.

SECTION TWO: THE FORMAL AND MATERIAL PRINCIPLES

as the incarnate Son of God for the express purpose of making atonement for sin and securing the eternal inheritance for the elect of God. Justification and sanctification, through union with the messianic Christ of promise, are spiritual realities for all true believers throughout the history of redemption. (For Christians, union with the *resurrected* Christ adds a new dimension to life in the Spirit. But this new covenant experience is wholly a matter of redemptive-historical placement in the divine scheme of things—what is our spiritual, eschatological life in the Spirit of Christ. Not even John the Baptist experienced the peculiarly post-Pentecostal, Christian reality introduced by Christ's coming into the world. Glorification at the end of the Age will unite all believers in the fullness of redemptive provision).

It is not until the time of Moses, mediator of the old covenant, that God reestablishes his *theocratic* rule among his people, this second time with Israel as recipient of God's electing grace, distinguishing Israel as holy to the Lord, separate from all the nations of the world. *Israel is both theocratic in constitution and typological of God's saving purpose in the world.* Israel's standing, her life in the land of earthly Canaan (a new Eden serving as symbol and type), is preliminary to the universal extension of the gospel in the eschatological age of new covenant church, arriving with the Spirit's outpouring on the Day of Pentecost. This Day, part of a complex of events associated with Christ's advent, marks a signal moment in redemptive history, separating two epochs of redemptive revelation. *The two canons of Scripture, old and new, give rise to the complexities of biblical interpretation, specifically, the matter of the relationship between the Old and New Testaments.* Alongside this hermeneutical challenge for the New Testament church is the task of explicating the rich, diverse, and complex typology associated with prophetic revelation under the old economy, including the introduction of the unique prophetic idiom, wherein the future Eschaton (the eternal, heavenly Kingdom) is portrayed in earthly, historical terms.[8]

Israel has been given the sabbath-ordinance as a peculiar observance among the people of God, not something to be practiced by all peoples.

---

8. Contra literalistic readings of the prophetic idiom. See the masterful exposition of Kline in *Glory in our Midst*. Elsewhere Kline comments: "The timing of the birth of the Bible was precisely conditioned; there were definite historical prerequisites for its appearance. If the Scriptural form of revelation was to be what it is—God's covenant addressed to the kingdom of his earthly people—then the Bible could have come into existence only when it did. Not earlier, for the appearance of Scripture having the character of kingdom-treaty required as its historical prelude the formation of a community peculiarly God's own and, beyond that, the development of this people to the stage of nationhood under God's lordship" (*The Structure of Biblical Authority*, 76).

God and Humanity

Likewise, the law of Moses, summed up in the Ten Commandments, belongs *exclusively* to the people of God, and most immediately to ancient theocratic Israel. It is not the law or constitution for all nations.[9] The sabbath is the sign and seal of the Covenant of Grace, affixed to the work and witness of God's people serving on behalf of God's spiritual kingdom. (The earthly, typological kingdom is unique in its establishment and purpose, propaedeutic and preparatory to the inauguration of the new covenant, at which time the Mosaic theocracy is brought to an end.) Furthermore, sabbath-observance differs under the old and new dispensations of redemptive grace. Whereas all is holy activity within the theocratic kingdom on earth, only kingdom-work (the spiritual mission of the church) is holy to the Lord in the age of the new covenant. Secular labor in the fields of medicine, technology, music, etc. are (in the non-theocratic context) common activities granted to all humankind. Consequently, under the new covenant God's people no longer enjoy a full day of rest, what was a typological anticipation of the eternal Sabbath, the consummate kingdom at the close of history. The temporal work of the cultivation and maintenance of the earth and of human society does not receive the promissory blessing of God (denoted by the sabbath-institution). Cultural activities, broadly defined, come to a close at the end of the age. At that time the eternal kingdom of God in the new heavens and new earth is sustained by the supernatural, consummate power of God, what is reserved for the Eschaton. Our diet will not be physical food, but the spiritual sustenance that God provides immediately through the Spirit. All creation will be subject to redeemed humanity's reign with Christ (Rom 8:17).

The Israelite theocracy consists of a kingdom of priests and kings ordered and governed by the covenantal institutions established by God through Moses.[10] Additionally, the prophetic institution is formalized and the call to repentance made all the more urgent in what is the time of preparation for the advent of the Messiah and for the establishment of the covenant in his shed-blood. The sacrificial work of Christ opens up a new and better way into the presence of God (see especially the argument presented in the Book of Hebrews). The constitution of Israel as the elect nation is set forth in the second giving of the law, in the Book of Deuteronomy,

---

9. The secular state, ordained by God, is a non-theocratic institution.

10. Geerhardus Vos observes: "The significance of the unique organization of Israel can be rightly measured only by remembering that the theocracy typified nothing short of the perfected kingdom of God, the consummate state of Heaven" (*Biblical Theology*, 126).

appropriately called the "Treaty of the Great King."[11] This covenantal document bears the distinguishing features of second-millennium Near Eastern treaties common to that period and civilization: preamble, historical prologue, stipulations, treaty sanctions for blessing and curse, and concluding arrangements for dynastic succession.

Tabernacle and Temple

The glory of God is revealed in the macro-and microcosmic levels of creation. However, we see the supreme imprint and reflection of God's glory in the manifestation of the Word incarnate, the Son of God who tabernacled among the sons of Israel. Christ Jesus is the exact representation of God's nature and glory (Heb 1:1–4 and John 1:1–18). Into his image the redeemed saints of God are refashioned and renewed. As part of the pedagogy of the Mosaic law and institutions, the earthly tabernacle symbolizes God's presence, his dwelling among men. The site of God's revelation and presence is holy ground; recipients of this divine revelation and theophany must image God's holiness and righteousness, if they are to share in God's likeness. It is in the context of the theocracy, the holy kingdom of priests and kings, that divine theophany manifests itself in the course of the history of redemptive revelation. (Divine theophany, subsequent to the establishment of the church of the new covenant, awaits the return of Christ in consummate glory at the end of the age).

Biblical theologian Geerhardus Vos explains: "The tabernacle is, as it were, a concentrated theocracy."[12] Within the tent of meeting are housed the two tablets of the law in the ark of the covenant, the holy vessels consecrated for use in the sacrificial offerings made to God, and other symbolic representations of God's presence and redemptive provision for theocratic Israel, all signifying in type the presence and sacrifice of the Lamb of God who was to come. So too, the garments of the priests are representative of the cosmic temple of God's glory manifested in the heavens above.[13]

11. Kline, *Treaty of the Great King*.
12. Vos, *Biblical Theology*, 148.

13. Kline explains: "In the broad parallelism that we have traced between the Genesis and Exodus creation episodes, Aaron's priestly investiture corresponds to the original creation of man in the image of God's Glory. The priestly vestments had the Glory-cloud for a pattern. This becomes readily apparent once we have recognized that the tabernacle too was a replica of the Glory-cloud, for there are striking similarities between the tabernacle and the priestly vestments. These similarities are made all the more conspicuous

GOD AND HUMANITY

The servants of the Lord—as holy priests and kings, as vassals of the Great King—are obliged to render (perfect) obedience to the commands of the Sovereign, the ruler of heaven and earth.

Settlement in the land of Canaan, occupation of the holy city of David (Mount Zion), prepares for the day when the glorious temple of Solomon, David's greater son, is erected. The (relative) permanency of the Solomonic temple gives added testimony to the fact that Israel is God's peculiar possession, sole inheritor of his saving grace and mercy through the mediation of Moses, God's servant. The splendor of Solomon's palace and temple, the residence of king and priest, is unsurpassed in the ancient world, according to the testimony of Scripture (1 Kgs 8:54–61; and chapter 10). But the pride of man jeopardizes the mission and witness of God's people as a theocratic nation. No sooner is the temple built that Solomon has designs to increase his power and visage by acquiring foreign wives, what was an abomination to the God of Israel. In this, Solomon proved to be less the king and servant than was his son David (1 Kgs 11:6).

Covenantal Engagement: The Word of the Prophets and Poets

The prophetic office is born in the postlapsum epoch of the history of humankind. (Prior to Adam's fall into sin, man occupied the twofold office of priest and king.) Prophecy as God's word of judgment, in blessing and in curse, arises out of the context of human sin and rebellion. As such, it bears a decidedly antithetical posture towards all human designs, cultic and cultural. From the earliest prophets up to John the Baptist, messenger of God's final ultimatum to the ancient theocratic people of Israel, God's intentions for the redemption and judgment of all things is revealed in the Word (i.e., Christ) and through the Spirit of Christ. Jesus, the Great Prophet of the covenant, realizes the supreme purpose and promise of God in the salvation of God's elect. It is he who enforces the eschatological sanctions of the covenant, already anticipated in Jesus' baptism by John.

---

in the Book of Exodus by the immediate juxtaposition there of the description of the tabernacle itself (Exod 25–27) and the instruction for the holy garments of those who ministered in the tabernacle (Exod 28). The tabernacle thus serves as an intermediate link in a remarkable symbolic series: the tabernacle is a replica of the Glory-Spirit and Aaron's vestments are a replica of the tabernacle—and thus also of the Glory-Spirit" (*Images of the Spirit,* 42).

Israel's disobedience necessitated the call for judicial proceedings: The latter-day prophets of Israel would serve as the agents of God's covenant lawsuit against his people, those who had broken his covenant and transgressed his laws. From the beginnings of the institution of the prophetic office, God raised up men uniquely suited to speak forth his will and purpose. As those conversant with the wisdom and counsel of God, these prophets were "caught up in the Spirit" (i.e., the Divine Counsel). The explanation of this unique experience is given in these words: "To be caught up in the Spirit was to be received into the divine assembly, the heavenly reality within the theophanic Glory-Spirit. The hallmark of the true prophet was that he had stood before the Lord of Glory in the midst of this deliberative council of angels."[14]

With regard to the poetical literature Kline comments: "The Psalter served broadly as a cultic instrument in the maintenance of a proper covenant relationship with Yahweh."[15] He further observes: "The Psalter's function in covenantal confession suggests that it may be regarded as an extension of the vassal's ratification response, which is found in certain biblical as well as extrabiblical covenants as part of the treaty text.... How completely appropriate, then, that the Psalter opens with an echo of the treaty blessings and curses and the declaration that judgment hinges on man's attitude towards the law of the covenant."[16] Much the same is true for the wisdom literature.[17]

The Fullness of Times: Paradise Remade

The New Testament scriptures are the account of redemption accomplished, chiefly a record of the birth, life, death, and resurrection of Christ as Israel's long-awaited Messiah, the true Servant of the Lord. Christ the Lord is the God-man, the Second Adam, who fulfills the messianic task of keeping covenant with God, his Father. In this capacity he is prophet, priest and king: his

---

14. Kline, *Images of the Spirit*, 58.

15. Ibid., 63. This thought is expressed in the opening Psalm in the collection of psalms, as throughout the Book of Psalms.

16. Ibid., 63, 64.

17. Kline remarks: "The central thesis of the wisdom books is that wisdom begins with the fear of Yahweh, which is to say that the way of wisdom is the way of the covenant." (*Images of the Spirit*, 64). He adds: "the function of the wisdom literature of the Old Testament is the explication of the covenant. One way it performs this is by translating the covenant stipulations into maxims and instructions regulative of conduct in the different areas of life and under it varying conditions" (ibid., 64–65).

mission is fulfilled in the transition from the initial state of humiliation (taking on human flesh for the purpose of the redemption of fallen humanity) to the state of exaltation (attainment of resurrection-Glory upon his ascension into heaven). Christ now intercedes on behalf of the elect as they are individually drawn to himself by the Spirit of God. There is an intimate relation between redemption accomplished (the work of Christ) and redemption applied (the work of the Spirit). Here is the difference between *historia salutis* and *ordo salutis*. Once again Kline, covenant theologian exemplar, remarks: "The relationship of Jesus, the divine paradigm prophet, to his image-bearing prophet-church of the new covenant involves a union beyond anything that obtained in the relationship between the Old Testament Angel-prophet and the Old Testament prophets fashioned in his likeness. The Lord Jesus and the church created in his image in the Spirit are identified with each other in the mystery of the union of the Head and the body."[18]

Union with Christ is the special benefit shared by all believers, before and after Christ's first advent. The difference is, however, that with the coming of Christ and the accomplishment of redemption, believers are now united with the *resurrected* Christ. Greater blessings flow to the saints of God resulting from this eschatological realization with respect to the history of salvation. Just as there is genuine progress in the history of redemption—the unfolding of the Covenant of Grace—so also is historical differentiation concerning the benefits received by way of union with (the resurrected) Christ. There is a greater sense of intimacy with God and a greater knowledge imparted as a result of the completed scriptures. The canon of the New Testament is regulative of life in the church of the new covenant, which differs in many and significant ways from life under of old (Mosaic) economy of redemption. The greatest difference resides in the transition from the age of shadows to the age of (semi-eschatological) fulfillment of the promises of God. Whereas kingdom and church were coextensive in the Israelite theocracy, now they are (once again) separate, but integrated, realities. The kingdom is the realm of Christ's spiritual rule and the church is the means of regulating the life of the saints in their historical circumstance. Additionally, there is the distinction between our cultic witness (the worship and mission of the church in the world) and our cultural activities (what is the engagement of believers and non-believers working side by side). The kingdom of God is distinct from cultural endeavors, what is "common" (not "holy"). The distinction between cultural and cultic is the distinction between common and holy.

18. Kline, *Images of the Spirit*, 96.

Section Two: The Formal and Material Principles

Lastly, the relation between Israel (the ancient, elect people of God) and the church (the spiritual organism as the seed of the woman, the seed of Christ) is brought into clearer light with the coming of Christ at his first advent. The crux of proper interpretation of the relationship between the Old and New Testaments is the place of typology in the unfolding of the history of the covenants.[19] Even here, there is the cataclysmic change between life in the semi-eschatology age of the Spirit (the age of the pentecostal church) that awaits the saints at the return of Christ in Glory: The realization of the heavenly, eternal Kingdom of Christ is the climax of the Covenant of Grace at the close of redemptive history. The Kingdom of God is not made by human hands; it is exclusively the consummate, everlasting bestowment of the Father which involves the entire cosmos. In the words of Kline: "For John sees a new world in which the cloud veil that had hidden the heavenly realm of God in his council from the eyes of mortal man is gone. Not only does the horizontal demarcation between the old temple and city disappear in the New Jerusalem, but the vertical distinction between heavenly and earthly temples as well."[20]

---

19. See Karlberg, "The Significance of Israel in Biblical Typology."
20. Kline, *Images of the Spirit*, 94.

Section Three

Departure from Historic Reformed Federalism

Chapter Five

Controversy within Present-Day Reformed Orthodoxy

Westminster Seminary in Philadelphia[1]

Introduction

ONCE SOUND INSTITUTIONS CAN and do err, resulting in the loss of theological and moral footing. This fact of church history is readily acknowledged by those committed to the preservation and propagation of Reformed orthodoxy in its essentials. The hard part for many is to recognize when and where deviation in the fundamentals of doctrine occurs in institutions once held in high regard. It is required, above all, that one remain faithful by taking a stand for truth, rather than demonstrating an unwillingness, a reluctance, or a refusal to speak out. Of course, there are those who will continue to support an institution for gain, whether personal or otherwise. Seduced by false rhetoric, charmed by personalities, threatened by retaliation or retribution of one kind or another, far too many individuals and organizations retreat from their obligation. Rather than "cross the line"—a line drawn by the miscreants themselves—many take shelter in silence and/or willing ignorance, oftentimes in varying combinations of the two.

Given the current upheaval within the Reformed community, the question arises: What accounts for the unending stream of articles, books, and "statements of faith"—institutional and organizational—upholding the

---

1. Previously published as "Master of Deception and Intrigue: Yet Another Glimpse into the Work and Psyche of Westminster Seminary."

Section Three: Departure from Historic Reformed Federalism

biblical doctrine of justification by faith alone (apart from good works)? Why the necessity for all these writings and reaffirmations? The answer is simply the fact that the biblical, Reformed doctrine of justification (more broadly, the doctrine of union with Christ) is under fierce assault from a variety of sources. Hence the urgency over the last four decades to restate and to defend the teaching of historic Protestant-Reformed orthodoxy. A second question to be asked is: *What is the chief source of defection within the evangelical-Reformed camp? And why the widespread reticence to name this source in academia? Should there be any doubt, let it be clearly said: the primary source of deviant teaching so prevalent today is Westminster Theological Seminary in Philadelphia.*[2] In the final instance it is fair to ask: Why are so many students leaving Westminster with views contrary to that of classic Reformed teaching, especially as regards the formal and the material principles of the Protestant Reformation (the doctrine of Scripture and the doctrine of justification by faith respectively)? What lies before us is not a minor skirmish, but a crisis of confidence and trust. What we are facing is an ever-widening spread of theological corruption, one that is severely impeding the work of the kingdom of Christ and witness to his Gospel of saving grace.

As noted often in my previous writings, Reformed theology is the theology of the covenants. This essay addresses two related elements in the system of doctrine—one that is primary, the other secondary. Denial of the first element results in a *radical* reinterpretation of covenant theology (leading to heterodoxy); a faulty understanding of the latter results in a defective view of the Covenant of Works, one nevertheless falling within the bounds of historic Reformed orthodoxy.[3] A leading feature of covenant theology (or federalism) is the antithesis between the two principles of inheritance/reward in the covenant(s) between God and his people: (1) *meritorious works* in the covenant established by God with humankind at creation, as well as in the temporal, symbolico-typical sphere of life in earthly Canaan during the Mosaic economy (the law serving as Israel's pedagogue), and with respect to the reconciling work of Christ as Second Adam (necessitating his meritorious obedience in the place of the sinner's transgression, covenant-breaking, and guilt); and (2) *saving faith* as instrumental in the reception of Christ's perfect righteousness imputed to the elect, and to them

2. *The Changing of the Guard*. Available online at www.trinityfoundation.org; republished in my *Gospel Grace*. This article serves as a sequel to this previous publication.

3. The first element pertains to the crucial law/gospel antithesis; the second to the misapplication of the biblical term "grace" to the preredemptive epoch (notably, the Covenant of Works).

alone. On this point of doctrine we meet up with the Protestant consensus (Lutheran and Reformed) concerning the law/grace antithesis. *Within the Reformed tradition this contrast has been uniquely applied to the covenantal structure of biblical history, redemptive and pre-redemptive.* And so it is that this doctrine of the covenants distinguishes the Reformed tradition from all other Protestant traditions. In modern times, the first major assault on this doctrine came from Karl Barth; in more recent times, in the work of Norman Shepherd and Richard Gaffin Jr. of Westminster Seminary.[4]

My doctoral study at Westminster in Philadelphia began under Shepherd. As early as matriculation into the M.Div. program, I was captivated by the work of Meredith G. Kline. Before long, I became instrumental in encouraging Professor Kline's return to Westminster to teach on a part-time basis (he was serving on the faculty of Gordon-Conwell Seminary at the time). In God's providence, my study at Westminster coincided with the outbreak of the Shepherd controversy on campus, first surfacing in 1975. Subsequent study at Westminster led to my master's thesis on Romans 7, giving special attention to the apostle Paul's interpretation of the Mosaic law. That was followed by the writing of my 1980 dissertation (*The Mosaic Covenant and the Concept of Works in Reformed Hermeneutics*). All told, these studies had an impact on the course of the Shepherd controversy. After careful study of the issues in dispute (including my studies on the doctrine of the covenants and justification), President Edmund Clowney reversed his prior, favorable stance toward Shepherd, and now began taking the steps necessary to have Shepherd removed from the faculty (*the decision having been based upon Shepherd's erroneous, heterodox teaching*). This complete about-face soon led to the writing of "Reasons and Specifications Supporting the Action of the Board of Trustees in Removing Professor Shepherd by the Executive Committee of the Board" (February 26, 1982). As part of the review process, I had been asked by the Committee charged with producing this document to provide a critique of Shepherd's theology on justification, election, and the covenants. Needless to say, these years at Westminster were exceedingly turbulent. Up to the current time, the situation remains much the same within the seminary community-at-large.

Prior to Clowney's reversal, he had attempted unsuccessfully to contain the crisis within the seminary, denouncing Shepherd's critics (notably,

---

4. See the prior volumes in my series of studies on covenant theology, wide-ranging and detailed, offering a comprehensive bibliography: *Covenant Theology in Reformed Perspective*; *Gospel Grace*; *Federalism and the Westminster Tradition*; and *Engaging Westminster Calvinism*.

the signers of the May 4, 1981 "Letter of Concern") for having sounded the alarm to outside scholars and pastors.[5] *In the end, in statements made in the Christian media and elsewhere, Clowney committed his biggest mistake by misleading the public regarding the true grounds for Shepherd's dismissal—downplaying Shepherd's false teaching, and emphasizing the need to distance the seminary from ongoing controversy.* This misjudgment was motivated, in part, by legal challenges raised by the theological accrediting agencies standing in the wings to protect the name and reputation of tenured professors. The same miscalculation—and for the same reason—was later repeated by President Peter Lillback and the seminary faculty in the dismissal of Peter Enns from the Old Testament department. Making matters more difficult in the prior case, President Clowney found Gaffin—Shepherd's staunchest supporter and the co-author, if not father, of the new teaching—to be a formidable force with which to contend. Since the time of Shepherd's dismissal, rupture within the faculty has never been repaired, and differences never resolved. Collegial estrangement continues to prevail to this day. Of course, the chief reason for ongoing conflict is fundamental disagreement in theological interpretation, involving issues of doctrinal substance.

Westminster East Today

Espousing anew a high view of Scripture—which members of the faculty have done throughout the history of the institution, even during its latter-day forage into novel and at times relativistic views of Scriptural interpretation (beginning in the mid-1970s[6])—Westminster today is hoping that its attempt to "hold the line" with regard to the authority and inerrancy of Scripture will overshadow the justification dispute, relegating the latter to a controversy in the distant past. *What has been up for grabs is the interpretation of Scripture, including radical reinterpretations.* Here we note five instances of such : (1) Harvie Conn's utilization of contextualization and its effect upon the (re)statement of modern-day Reformed dogmatics;

---

5. The major impetus for the turnaround on the part of the President of the seminary was dissemination of this May letter signed by forty-five theologians and pastors voicing objection to Shepherd's exoneration. See the literature on the Shepherd controversy for additional details and developments, cited in my previous books.

6. It was during the days of the Shepherd controversy that faculty members were intent upon teaching freely their own views, without others looking critically over their shoulders; support for Shepherd entailed an implicit pass to teach without restraint or criticism from colleagues.

(2) Peter Enns' allegorical interpretations in portions of recorded biblical history (building upon the prior work of Raymond Dillard and Tremper Longman);[7] (3) Moisés Silva's promotion of redaction criticism, which in this instance amounts to a variation on multiple theological perspectives such as that advocated by John Frame; (4) the employment of Barthian doctrine (specifically, the notion of the priority of grace to law resulting in denial of the traditional Protestant Law/Gospel antithesis) by Norman Shepherd, Richard Gaffin, Sinclair Ferguson, David Garner, Peter Lillback, Carl Trueman, William Edgar, and Scott Oliphant (to name only some of Westminster's faculty); and (5) Frame's invention of multi-perspectivalism as a replacement for traditional Reformed systematics, resulting in a change in theology and methodology.[8] All of these streams feed into the single delta, the theological watershed known as New School Westminster.

In the February 8, 2014 issue of *World* magazine, P&R Publishing advertised two new, "seminal" books, *Thy Word is Still Truth* (edited by Lillback and Gaffin), and Frame's *Systematic Theology*.[9] With regard to the latter, the advertisement claims: "This magisterial opus—at once biblical, clear, cogent, readable, accessible, and practical—summarizes the mature thought of one of the most important and original Reformed theologians of the last hundred years." Together these two books once again bring into view the formative principles of the Protestant Reformation, the doctrine of Scripture and the doctrine of justification by faith alone, two of many crucial doctrines in Reformed dogmatics. In Frame's book, the author takes yet another occasion to castigate Shepherd's critics; he proceeds then to instruct the Reformed world how to think theologically.[10] To be sure, Frame's methodology and doctrinal formulation do find a following among

---

7. Enns, like his colleagues in the Old Testament department, claimed to uphold "inerrancy." The problem lay in his *(re)interpretation* of Scripture.

8. This methodology has enabled Frame to be ambiguous, vague, and evasive on certain issues, waffling on others. See the exchange between Frame and Karlberg on the Trinity Foundation's website, *Trinity Review* (2001) at www.trinityfoundation.org. For further analysis of Frame, see my "On the Theological Correlation of Divine and Human Language: A Review Article," and my "John Frame and the Recasting of Van Tilian Apologetics: A Review Article."

9. *World* magazine, 33. Lillback and Gaffin Jr., eds., *Thy Word is Still Truth*; and Frame, *Systematic Theology*.

10. Frame characteristically assumes a posture of humility, while castigating his critics in the strongest of words (at times when he is not justified to doing so).

SECTION THREE: DEPARTURE FROM HISTORIC REFORMED FEDERALISM

some, but his work nevertheless remains highly controversial and highly contentious.[11]

Systematic Theology: An Introduction to Christian Belief[12] is a distillation of Frame's theological ruminations over the course of his teaching career (billed as his *magnum opus*). As has been pointed out by many, Frame's book and approach are subjective, amounting to a subtle, and not so subtle, attempt to repudiate traditional Reformed dogmatics at a number of key points in the theological system. His methodology can only yield at best an "introduction," not a summary or compendium of Reformed, biblical teaching. The author prides himself on his own thinking—free of what he sees to be the dogmatism of the "traditionalists"—with token regard for historic Reformed theology on several critical points of doctrine. Curious at this point in the controversy is the ambivalence and the duplicity concerning Shepherd's distinctive teaching, what Frame regards as mere quibbling over formulation. *Frame does not regard Shepherd's theology to be unorthodox, rather that is ascribed to the thinking of his critics.*[13] Frame substitutes his multi-perspectivalism, his many triads of *theological applica-*

---

11. Frame's attempt to answer his critics is evident in both the design and the content of his *festschrift*, where Frame hand-picked his contributors to commend, promote, and defend his work; see *Speaking the Truth in Love*. At Westminster Seminary's "Alumni and Friends Lunch" conducted during the 2013 annual meeting of the Evangelical Theological Society, Gaffin addressed the topic of biblical inerrancy. He was joined on this occasion by Frame. The seminary is striving to put the best face on the school in the presence of ongoing criticism from various quarters and on several issues of doctrinal import.

12. The Westminster Bookstore announces on its website (www.wtsbooks.com): "*Systematic Theology* is the culmination and creative synthesis of John Frame's writing on, teaching about, and studying of the Word of God. This magisterial opus—at once biblical, clear, cogent, readable, accessible, and practical—summarizes the mature thought of one of the most important and original Reformed theologians of the last hundred years. It will enable you to see clearly how the Bible explains God's great, sweeping plan for mankind." Frame's study has won numerous accolades from evangelical theologians—endorsements provided by the publisher at the opening of the book (comprising twenty pages preceding the title page). J. I. Packer provides the Foreword in which he denounces critics of the author—not surprising from one who has himself abandoned, in places, traditional Protestant-Reformed teaching (see, in particular, Packer's role in writing the ecumenical document "Evangelicals and Catholics Together: The Christian Mission in the Third Millennium," 1994).

13. Concerning the doctrine of justification, Frame maintains that "Shepherd reflected remarkable insight into the teaching of Scripture" (*Systematic Theology*, 975). And with regard specifically to the covenantal structure of biblical revelation, pre-and post-fall, Frame concedes that his argument is "dependent on Shepherd." Here he cites Shepherd's *The Call of Grace*, which publication Gaffin had commended in glowing terms on the book's back cover (*Systematic Theology*, 71 n.18).

tion (which includes the believer's experiential appropriation of the Word), for the unique Scripture principle (which identifies Scripture as *self-interpreting*). Frame's approach has a leveling effect on the authority of Scripture and human understanding of the Word. Frame employs a (new) version of church tradition of his own liking. Frame's lengthy work lacks adequate interaction with the broader theological literature, preferring highly selective citations to works addressing issues with which the author disputes and with theologians with whom he disagrees (notably those within the Westminster community). Frame is novel in his approach and in many of his conclusions; as a whole, the book is idiosyncratic and out of step with traditional dogmatics (which is the intended goal of Frame's theologizing).

The battle for truth and honesty at Westminster has been uphill all the way for those "outside" the citadel. And new, fresh blood on the faculty has, likewise, been incapable of extricating the seminary from its errors and missteps. Regrettably, one cannot look to Gregory Beale's recently published *magnum opus*, titled *A New Testament Biblical Theology: The Unfolding of the Old Testament in the New*,[14] for help sorting out the long-standing, divisive issues concerning the justification dispute at Westminster (even though, to his credit, Beale did take an aggressive stand against the views of Peter Enns on biblical inerrancy and interpretation). Beale's hesitant and reserved comments in this volume further confuse and compound the grievance against the seminary faculty in an ever widening dispute.[15]

Westminster East and West: Similarities and Differences

Firstly, despite common roots extending back to the founding of Westminster by J. Gresham Machen in 1929—both campuses claiming to be following Machen's vision and theological convictions and to be bound by the teachings of the Westminster Standards—the two have largely parted ways. This in itself is indicative of grave problems in theological understanding and genuine commitment to the Reformed confessions. As noted in the introduction, discord and estrangement continue to prevail, ever since the

---

14. Grand Rapids: Baker, 2011.

15. For additional critique and analysis, see my *Engaging Westminster Calvinism*, chapter two ("Conflating Faith and Works in Final Judgment/Justification: The Teaching of New School Westminster").

SECTION THREE: DEPARTURE FROM HISTORIC REFORMED FEDERALISM

days of Shepherd's dismissal from the faculty.[16] The action by President Clowney and the Board of Trustees did not bring about a fruitful, lasting resolution by any measure of assessment. Secondly, despite the opposition of the two faculties on matters relating to the doctrine of justification by faith, union with Christ, and the Covenant of Works (to name only a few), Westminster West's position on justification is compromised by endorsement of Gaffin's alleged "orthodoxy." As a consequence, the faculty of Westminster West sits precariously on the fence in the ongoing battle over sovereign, justifying grace (in contrast to inheritance/reward by "the works of the law"). The faculty is fully cognizant of Gaffin's dominant role in the Shepherd controversy and his own problematic (even deviant) formulations. *Never has Gaffin publically disassociated or distanced himself from Shepherd's theology—at least not to any significant or meaningful degree. The true state of affairs is this: Gaffin's position has not changed substantively in any way (contrary to all false, misleading reports).*[17]

---

16. William Dennison, a member of the faculty of Covenant College and Northwest Seminary (a hotbed for anti-Klineans), offers several barbs against the theological position of David VanDrunen, illustrative of the war raging within the broader seminary community. Dennison has frequently aired opinions against members of the faculty at Westminster in California, including his dislike for all who oppose the distinctive teaching of New School Westminster (in Philadelphia). In his "Review of VanDrunen's *Natural Law and the Two Kingdoms* (349–70), Dennison asserts: "The breadth of VanDrunen's volume and the scholarly analysis, however, remains elementary and exhibits a number of shortcomings" (351). Overall, a "shallow interdisciplinary study" (352). Dennison concludes the review by warning: "anyone intending serious scholarly use of his volume should proceed with grave caution. . . . We still await, therefore, a definitive work on *Natural Law and the Two Kingdoms* in light of Reformed orthodoxy; at best, VanDrunen's study serves as a minor footnote to any sincere historical study of the subject" (369). Just one more barometer on the dampening climate hanging over the Westminster community.

17. After years of debate and conflict, Shepherd, Gaffin, and Frame came to acknowledge the active obedience of Christ in the procurement of salvation. Yet this element in their theology remains meaningless, given their rejection of the traditional Lutheran-Reformed antithesis between law and grace—the former being obedience to God's commands, on which basis covenant reward is earned in the original Covenant of Works; the latter being inheritance by faith alone (apart from "good works"). It is the contention of Shepherd, Gaffin, and Frame—and many others schooled in their teaching—that the classic law/grace doctrine is Lutheran, not genuinely Reformed. Gaffin's 2006 study, *"By Faith, Not by Sight"* has just been republished and released by P&R in March of 2014. In the "Preface to the Second Edition" Gaffin writes: "The revisions in this edition are not extensive, though occasionally they are substantive. In a number of places I have rewritten to be as clear as I can, particularly in light of criticisms of the first edition. At several points I have addressed specific criticisms" (xvii). Both Gaffin and Frame are well aware of the criticisms of their work, yet they remain adamant in their repudiation

Frame found himself unwelcome at Westminster California, and when the opportunity came to leave for greener pastures at Reformed Theological Seminary (RTS) in Orlando he was eager to go. Here he found a safe, hospitable environment in which to carry on his theological work. The faculty at RTS proved to be very supportive and nurturing. Since leaving Westminster, Frame has directed numerous criticisms in his writings against several faculty members on the Escondido campus on a number of critical issues. Echoing the stance of many in censuring opponents of Shepherd and Gaffin, repeated attempts are made to silence all opposition, either by misrepresentation, false caricature, or cover-up—ignoring as far as possible valid criticism as if it did not exist or was unworthy of engagement. Both Westminster East and West are culpable for mishandling the controversy and deceiving the public; any difference in culpability is merely one of degree. As in the case of Princeton Seminary in the early twentieth century, the tide has changed for Westminster, most notably in Philadelphia. All this has resulted in a loss of confidence, trust, and respect for the faculty and the institution(s). Only by taking a firm stand will Westminster West earn the title of "courageous Calvinists," to which it so eagerly aspires. Until such time, the future of historic orthodox Calvinism in America is highly uncertain; what prevails is the further erosion of truth among the churches of the Reformation.[18]

Westminster Seminary in California was founded as a seminary-in-exile (a residence largely for opponents of Shepherd who were teaching on the Philadelphia campus).[19] The plan was to keep the two campuses together institutionally, but over time that relationship was severed. Redeemer Theological Seminary (Dallas, Texas) is yet another, more recent offshoot of the Philadelphia campus. It was founded originally in 1999 as an extension campus, but the school obtained independent status in 2009 (after the dismissal of Peter Enns from the Philadelphia faculty in 2008).

---

of the classic Protestant-Reformed Law/Gospel antithesis. See my combined review of Paul A. Rainbow's *The Way of Salvation* and Richard B. Gaffin's *"By Faith, Not by Sight,"* republished in *Engaging Westminster Calvinism*.

18. Compare David F. Wells, *God in the Whirlwind*, growing out of a multi-volume analysis of Protestant "evangelicalism" more broadly, beginning with *No Place for Truth*. Wells demonstrates a masterful grasp of the present-day theological canvas.

19. While serving on the Philadelphia faculty, Jay Adams pioneered "nouthetic" counseling; that discipline offered little help to the faculty in the days of the turbulent upheaval brought about by the Shepherd controversy. Such tumult led to the estrangement of many faculty members and friends. Subsequently, Adams relocated to the Escondido campus in 1983 (along with other faculty members who opposed Shepherd's teaching).

Section Three: Departure from Historic Reformed Federalism

Among the faculty members are Dan McCartney (unwavering supporter of Enns), Clair Davis (defender of Shepherd), and Sinclair Ferguson (whose own work has been shaped in significant ways by Gaffin's theology).

Westminster's Impact on the Evangelical-Reformed Churches

The teachings of Westminster Seminary, a leading Reformed academic institution, have had an enormous impact upon the churches. Over the years, the seminary has made inroads into the Orthodox Presbyterian Church, the Presbyterian Church in America (including its denominational seminary, Covenant), the United Reformed Churches of North America, and other institutions like Mid-America Reformed Seminary. The latest effort has been taken by the Presbytery of the Northwest (OPC) calling for a denominational study of the works-inheritance principle in the Mosaic Covenant.[20] The central issue at stake here is, once again, the Protestant-Reformed Law/Gospel antithesis.

Denial of the tutelary works-inheritance principle functioning within the Mosaic economy (properly restricted to the typological, earthly sphere

---

20. See the website, "The Study of the Mosaic Covenant" (https://sites.google.com/site/mosaiccovenant/home). A lengthy paper of ninety-seven pages was submitted to presbyters at the April 2013 Stated Meeting, in hopes of persuading the Presbytery to overture the General Assembly, calling for a denominational study to evaluate sharply differing views on the Mosaic Covenant and to help resolve deep-seated conflict and disagreement within the church. A second, subsequent paper written by three former students of Westminster in California was made available to these same presbyters prior to the September 2013 meeting of Presbytery advocating the republication view (countering the position of the first paper). In my judgment, the former distorts both the history and the import of the Shepherd-Gaffin controversy. The proposal being adopted, the Overture reads: "The Presbytery of the Northwest respectfully overtures the 81st General Assembly of the Orthodox Presbyterian Church to establish a study committee to examine and give its advice as to whether and in which particular senses the concept of the Mosaic Covenant as a republication of the Adamic Covenant is consistent with the doctrinal system taught in the confessional standards of the Orthodox Presbyterian Church."

In a review of Ryan M. McGraw's *Christ's Glory, Your Good*, Geoffrey Willour comments: "Of particular significance for contemporary discussions within churches of the confessional Reformed and Presbyterian family (including the OPC) are McGraw's emphasis on the eternal covenant of redemption, his exposition of the bi-covenantal structuring of God's historical dealings with mankind (i.e., the covenant of works and the covenant of grace), his emphasis on the importance and centrality of union with Christ, and his defense of the active obedience of Christ, showing how Christ by his active obedience fulfills the covenant of works on behalf of his elect" (*New Horizons*, 21–22).

of life in Canaan) not only entails a blatant misreading of the Old and New Testaments, but also the imposition of an erroneous interpretation of the covenants spanning pre-redemptive and redemptive history. At issue also is a faulty conception of the principle of federal headship pertaining to the First and Second Adams. The biblical idea of meritorious reward in the Covenant of Works, that is, reward based upon Adam's fulfillment of the requirement of God's law (whereby human obedience earns the blessing of God after a period of probationary testing), is essential for maintaining the parallel drawn by the apostle Paul with respect to the two Adams. The reward that would have been granted by God to Adam, had he fulfilled his covenantal, legal obligation, would obviously not have been won by a substitutionary, divine representative as is the case in the Covenant of Grace (wherein the exclusive ground of eternal life is the perfect righteousness of Christ, the Second Adam, imputed to the elect). Inheritance by works—contrasting with inheritance by grace—is required by God's covenantal law first given to humankind; entailed here is the crucial Law/Gospel antithesis. Discussion within the Orthodox Presbyterian Church, and elsewhere, will not advance until the Shepherd-Gaffin heterodoxy is clearly and honestly identified—and decisively excised. Instead of majoring on the minor (what I have identified above as the "secondary element" in the doctrine of the Covenant of Works, namely, construal of God's covenantal reward for obedience as a gift of grace, rather than meritorious accomplishment on the part of the First Adam, had he kept God's command), full attention must be directed to Gaffin's repudiation of the classic Protestant-Reformed law/grace contrast. To do anything less is to obscure and cover over what is central in this four-decade-old controversy regarding justification by faith.

Biblically defined, the term "grace"—fundamental and all-determinative in this dispute—refers *exclusively* to sovereign, electing grace ("saving" grace, the *only* grace to which the Bible refers). Application of this term as a qualification for the way in which Adam would have received the consummate blessing of God and reward for successful completion of probation under the original Covenant of Works (before Adam's fall into sin) has proved not only to be confusing, but has opened the door to erroneous interpretation of the two-fold covenants (works and grace). *The time has come in the history of orthodox federalism (that is, Reformed dogmatics) for ambiguity and misformulation to be acknowledged and finally resolved—by modifying and correcting the teaching of the church to conform to Scripture.*

Section Three: Departure from Historic Reformed Federalism

Failing to do so will only perpetuate division within the academy and the churches, division that in the final analysis is unwarranted and unnecessary.

On other fronts, objection had been formally raised against the decision of the Session of Tenth Presbyterian Church in Philadelphia for having Gaffin speak in March 2014 at The Boice Center, a ministry of Tenth Church.[21] (Gaffin's topic was "Inerrancy and the Self-Witness of the Bible." Gaffin changed his lecture to the following: "Inerrancy: Adam and the Gospel.") The response of the church elders was to consult Cornerstone OPC where Gaffin worships and has an active hand in the affairs of the congregation.[22] Cornerstone's answer was to reassure inquisitors that Gaffin was unhesitatingly sound and orthodox. Likewise, in March 2014, John Piper, popular Baptist pastor and teacher, was selected as the speaker for Westminster's Seventh Annual Gaffin Lecture in Theology, Culture, and Missions at the seminary, and also as special speaker at Proclamation Presbyterian Church in Bryn Mawr, Pennsylvania (where Peter Lillback is *pastor emeritus* and David Garner serves currently as a pastor of teaching). Piper's topic at Proclamation was "Suffering and the Supremacy of Christ." All this to say, this was a strategic move on the part of the seminary, given the fact that Piper's views on covenant and justification are wholly in sync with the teaching of New Westminster.[23] Piper's visit would potentially galvanize the Westminster community in the Philadelphia area and help secure maximum support for the school. The controversy regarding the biblical doctrine of Scripture and justification by faith is not just a problem isolated to the Westminster (Reformed) community. It is deeply divisive within the Evangelical Theological Society. One should be reminded that

---

21. The deviant teaching of Westminster Seminary was introduced long ago to Tenth Presbyterian Church by its senior pastor, James M. Boice, who had befriended Sinclair Ferguson (now a teaching fellow at Ligonier Ministries). Boice came to denounce the Reformed doctrine of the "Covenant of Works." Subsequently, neither Phil Ryken, Boice's immediate successor, nor the current senior pastor, Liam Goligher, nor any other members of the pastoral/ministerial staff, past or present (most of whom were trained at Westminster), have ever distanced Tenth from Westminster's new teaching.

22. For more insight into Cornerstone Orthodox Presbyterian Church, see Stephen M. Cunha, *The Emperor Has No Clothes*. Gaffin left Calvary OPC in Glenside—across the street from Westminster Seminary—to help organize Cornerstone and, at the same time, to seek ways to alleviate tensions within the seminary community where possible. Arthur Kuschke, a member of the Glenside congregation, kept a very close eye on all developments stemming from the Shepherd dispute. See histories of the controversy for additional background on Kuschke's active and highly significant role in opposing Shepherd's teaching both in the seminary and the OPC.

23. Karlberg, *John Piper on the Christian Life*.

adherence to the formal principle of the Protestant Reformation, historically understood, is one of the few doctrinal planks of the society. Needless to say, the organization has been unable to hold all members to this pledge (Enns being one example). The title of Enn's paper at the 2013 annual meeting of the Evangelical Theological Society was "Abandoning Inerrancy Is Necessary for Evangelical Integrity."[24] The Society serves as a useful gauge of present-day trends within Protestant "evangelicalism."

One of the most respected and influential popularizers of Reformed theology today is R.C. Sproul, Sr. In his newly released book, *Everyone's a Theologian*,[25] we read contradictory teaching on the Covenant of Works, teaching that has become all too familiar within Reformed scholarship, teaching that can readily lead to a false understanding of the relation between faith and good works in the article of justification. Sproul rightly distinguishes the works-covenant from the grace-covenant by explaining that "the destiny of the human race was decided on the basis of performance, specifically on the basis of the obedience of Adam and Eve. If they remained obedient, they would enter into an eternal state of blessedness. However it they failed to conform to that stipulation, then they would die, along with their descendants."[26] *Rightly understood, this is nothing other than the works-merit principle functioning with respect to human obtainment of the promised, covenanted reward (wherein God freely obligates himself to bless, not curse, humankind represented in Adam on grounds of perfect obedience to the law of God).*

Unfortunately, this crucial teaching concerning the law/grace antithesis is undermined by Sproul in his following remarks: "Another misunderstanding comes from how we identify the two covenants. Because the first is called 'the covenant of works' and the other is called 'the covenant of grace,' we tend to think that the first covenant had no grace." Sproul speculatively contends that "for God to enter into any covenant with a creature, to give any promise to us whatsoever under any conditions, is in itself a gracious act. God is not required to promise His creatures anything" (123). This entails an erroneous assessment of the biblical covenants, one that can only jeopardize the

---

24. Currently, Enns is on the faculty of Eastern University.

25. As an introduction, Sproul's concise volume is vastly superior to Frame's in laying out the fundamentals of the faith-and does so far more reliably.

26. *Everyone's a Theologian*, 123. The probationary test hinged on Adam's "one act of righteousness:" Eve would either affirm or deny the lordship of God (including either upholding or undermining the role and responsibility given to Adam as federal head in the original Covenant of Works).

Section Three: Departure from Historic Reformed Federalism

law/grace antithesis Sproul himself is eager to maintain.²⁷ At the opening of history with the establishment of the covenant with Adam, federal head of all humanity, God pledged to bind himself to this covenant, one of his own making, one which he *freely* ordained. God was not obliged to do so. *To be sure, the covenant at creation was an act of divine condescension and beneficence, but it was not "gracious." That term is descriptive exclusively of redemptive covenant (the so-called "Covenant of Grace").* Biblical interpreters cannot have it both ways.²⁸ Theological systematization demands consistency

---

27. Sproul was a critic of the Shepherd theology, one of the signers of the now historic May 4, 1981 letter sent out to a broader Reformed audience objecting to the seminary's exoneration of Shepherd. With regard to the Mosaic Covenant, Sproul acknowledges the works-principle in operation, a principle antithetical to that of saving grace (functioning in the new covenant). He explains that "we are saved by grace, and grace comes through the person and work of Christ. . . . He came into the world and placed Himself under the stipulations of the original covenant of works. . . . Justification is through faith in Christ alone because Christ alone fulfilled the covenant of works" (164). The doctrine of the covenants and the role of Old Testament typology are major features of Reformed Biblical theology, a discipline fully compatible with systematics when the two are rightly formulated. Graeme Goldsworthy in *Christ-Centered Biblical Theology: Hermeneutical Foundations and Principles* offers an alternative to the views of Geerhardus Vos, the father of Biblical theology in the twentieth century, and Edmund P. Clowney, a champion at Westminster of the Biblical, redemptive-historical approach. In making his case Goldsworthy rejects the doctrine of the Covenant of Works. This has profound implications for biblical and systematic theology, two mutually compatible methodologies, both essential in explicating the full teaching of Scripture.

28. Sproul's elaboration on the difference between justice, on the one hand, and grace and mercy, on the other, leads him to assert (correctly) that "grace is not justice. Grace and mercy are outside the category of justice, but they are not inside the category of injustice" (*Everyone's a Theologian*, 69). In defining the term "grace" in the later section of the book dealing with soteriology, Sproul explains: "At the outset, we must distinguish between grace and justice. Justice is something that is earned or merited by our works" (163). It is necessary here to underscore that this earning on the part of the creature made in God's image is based wholly upon God's covenant arrangement established at creation—what federalists call reward *ex pacto*. "So justice is related to a standard of merit. In contrast, grace is undeserved; that is, it is not earned or merited. Rather, grace is given freely by God. He is not obligated or required to give it" (163).

For additional clarification it must be said that the grace freely given to sinners—something not required of God—is wholly descriptive of the Covenant of Grace. Though the first covenant at creation, the Covenant of Works, was freely bestowed (as an act of divine condescension and beneficence), it was not an act of "grace," which pertains exclusively to God's redemptive provision. Had Adam obeyed the command of the Lord in that first covenant, he would have justly earned the promised reward of eternal, eschatological life (leading to consummate transformation into the image of the Glory-Spirit, who initially hovered over the creation of the world as earthly habitat and the creation of humankind as God's image-bearer). Theological terminology must conform to the

and clarity of expression. Above all, my good friend and respected expositor of the Scriptures, R.C., should know this well.

Where Now Do Federal Confessionalists Stand?

The legacy Westminster has bequeathed to the Reformed world, notably to the Orthodox Presbyterian Church and the Presbyterian Church in America, is found wanting. Widespread theological confusion and misunderstanding brought about by the Shepherd-Gaffin teaching finds its roots in formulations by the early Reformed federalists, conveyed most immediately to students of the seminary chiefly through the work of John Murray, Westminster's leading systematician in the early days of the seminary.[29] One of the most recent engagements with the ongoing dispute over justification and the covenants appears in *The Westminster Theological Journal*, in an article entitled "Missing, Presumed Misclassified: Hugh Binning (1627–1653), the Lost Federal Theologian," written by Donald John MacLean (*WTJ* 75 [2013] 261–78). Here MacLean sets out to counter the dominant Barth-Torrance critique of scholastic federalism (specifically, criticism of the law/grace, or Law/Gospel contrast). At the heart of the dispute is the understanding held by some regarding (*non-saving*) grace as the basis for (*unmerited*) reward in the Covenant of Works. Wherein precisely does "grace" and "Gospel-grace" differ with respect to the way of receiving the inheritance promised in the first covenant with Adam, the federal head (upon successful completion of probationary testing, resulting in confirmation in righteousness and the securing of life everlasting)? *Crucial with regard to this question in Reformed covenant theology is the essential and vital idea of meritorious reward (as that informs Christ's work as Second Adam, and as regards the operation of the works-principle in the Mosaic economy).* Without it, there is no Law/Gospel antithesis. Biblically defined, the theological term "grace" applies *exclusively* to redemptive promise and reward. Within scholastic Reformed federalism

---

teaching of Scripture, not church tradition (dogma) which conveys at times rationalistic speculations. There is and continues to be progress in doctrinal formulation within the history of the Christian church; such progress entails *better apprehension* of the Scriptures as God's self-revelation, *not new truths*. This is the result of the Spirit's illumination of the Word in the hearts and minds of believers.

29. Helyer, *The Witness of Jesus, Paul and John* expresses indebtedness to Karlberg for his critique of covenant theology at Westminster Seminary, notably that of Murray. Compare the studies by Jeong Koo Jeon, *Covenant Theology; Covenant Theology and Justification by Faith;* and *Calvin and the Federal Vision*.

the notion of (pre-redemptive) "grace" as the basis, reason, or justification for the reward promised to Adam in the Covenant of Works is foreign to the witness of Scripture. Perpetuation of this un-Scriptural terminology with respect to the pre-Fall covenant only perpetuates a defective interpretation of the divine covenants and of justification by faith alone (apart from the "works of the law"). Covenantal inheritance is either by faith in the Covenant of Grace or by works in the Covenant of Works (broken by Adam's fall into sin). In Christ the promise has been secured for elect humanity, necessitating the imputation of his perfect righteousness to those justified by grace through faith.

Regrettably, MacLean promotes the view held by Samuel Rutherford (and Hugh Binning), "that God showed grace to Adam in establishing this covenant [the original covenant of works] with him. He believed that Adam could have served God perfectly forever and never earned a right to confirmation of eternal life. Therefore God's promise was to reward obedience above what it merited and, for Rutherford, is demonstrated that even the covenant of works contained grace.... This acknowledgment of grace in the covenant of works did not prevent Rutherford from sharply distinguishing that grace from the grace shown in the *foedus gratiae,* stating that there was 'no Gospel-Grace' in the covenant of works" (274–75). The author informs his readers that Binning would agree with Rutherford's understanding. "Indeed, Binning stated that 'it was Paul's great business in preaching, to ride marches between the covenant of grace, and the covenant of works'" (275n.99). This doctrine of pre-Fall grace is the result of abstract speculation on the part of federalist expositors, whether seventeenth-century or contemporary.[30] *In the case of Shepherd and Gaffin, this feature or element*

---

30. Andrew Woolsey's 1988 dissertation *Unity and Continuity in Covenantal Thought* (Glasgow University) published in 2012 by Reformation Heritage Books is somewhat dated, in that it does not interact with literature since 1988 (hence, no analysis of the Shepherd-Gaffin school of interpretation now requisite in such studies). The author holds essentially to the position of John Murray on the covenants, though he does not call for a "recasting" of covenant theology as Murray had done. For a critique of Woolsey's book similar to mine, see Andrew J. Martin's book review of Woolsey in *WTJ* 75 (2013) 425–428. Commendable also is Mark Kim's analysis of Michael Horton's federalism in relation to this present-day controversy (see "Michael Horton's Covenant Theology as a Defense of Reformation Theology in the Context of Current Discussions"). Among recent publications upholding the two-fold covenants, we take note of these: Daniel W. McManigal, *Encountering Christ in the Covenants*; Mark Brown, *Christ and the Condition*; and the republication of Johannes Cocceius, *The Doctrine of the Covenant and Testament of God,* translated by Casey Carmichael. For interaction with Beach's reading of Johannes Cocceius and Francis Turretin, see my "Recovering the Mosaic Covenant as

of doctrine has become the foil for radical reinterpretation of the Reformed doctrine of the covenants.[31]

To be sure, there is pressing need to correct misformulations based on rationalistic speculation. As superb as it is, we must always remember that the *Westminster Confession of Faith* is not an infallible document. It remains subject to modification and clarification in light of the teachings of Scripture. In the earliest days, American Presbyterians (with biblical justification) altered the confessional understanding on the matter of church-state relations. The time has surely come to correct the confessional understanding of "voluntary condescension" (specifically directed against the notion of human meritorious reward).[32] For those denying the "merit" principle operative in the Mosaic and creation covenants, what biblical basis remains for upholding the crucial the Law/Gospel antithesis? We see where its renunciation has led Shepherd and Gaffin, primary crafters of the New Westminster theology.

Where there is greater light, there is greater accountability. Rather than continuing its campaign of misleading and deceiving the public (with all the intrigue that tactic conjures up), the seminary is obliged to respond openly and straightforwardly to her critics. Nothing less will bring about renewed credibility, confidence, and respect for leadership in the church and in the academy. As sounded by Robert Godfrey years ago, there is (and remains) a theological *and* moral problem at Westminster. The offense has only been compounded in the intervening decades, cementing a culture of deceit. For too long, deception and intrigue have ruled the day at Westminster;

Law and Gospel: J. Mark Beach, John H. Sailhamer, and Jason C. Meyer as Representative Expositors," *EvQ* 83/3 (2011) 233–50, republished in *Engaging Westminster Calvinism*, chapter three.

31. For detailed elaboration, see my *Gospel Grace*.

32. "The distance between God and the creature is so great, that although reasonable creatures do owe obedience unto Him as their Creator, yet they could never have any fruition of Him as their blessedness and reward, but by some *voluntary condescension* on God's part, which He has been pleased to express by way of covenant" (WCF 7.1). "We cannot by our best works merit pardon of sin, or eternal life at the hand of God, *by reason of the great disproportion that is between them and the glory to come; and the infinite distance that is between us and God*, whom, by them, we can neither profit, nor satisfy for the debt of our former sins, but when we have done all we can, we have done but our duty, and are unprofitable servants: and because, as they are good, they proceed from His Spirit, and as they are wrought by us, they are defiled, and mixed with so much weakness and imperfection, that they cannot endure the severity of God's judgment" (WCF 16.5). *Emphasis added.* For further analysis, see especially my *Covenant Theology in Reformed Perspective*, which builds upon my doctoral study.

Section Three: Departure from Historic Reformed Federalism

such has become the seminary's *modus operandi*. What we find are false shepherds leading the blind, and an institution bearing a similar cast to the Church at Rome in terms of theological and moral corruption.[33] Christian institutions are to be held to the highest standards, especially seminaries which train and prepare future pastors and church leaders. Of course, there is room for mistakes, followed by correction: Human error is part of the fallen human condition, and repentance is a work of God's grace. Public offences must be publicly righted. This is Westminster's solemn duty and calling. But after four long decades, the replacement of faculty and board members who do not carry soiled baggage may be the only remedy for the school. Professor Meredith Kline once remarked that it would be better to close the doors of the seminary than have the current state of affairs persist. Wise judgment from an extraordinarily gifted, humble, and godly servant of God, who gave so freely and generously of himself—evidence of his love for Christ and his church. Kline bore faithful testimony to the truth of God's Word for those who have ears to hear what the Spirit says in the Scriptures. We need more servants of this caliber, giftedness, and devotion in the church and in the academy today.

---

33. *Secrets of the Vatican*, a PBS *Frontline* documentary aired on February 25, 2014, gives a window into the operation and maneuverings of some Christian institutions, in this instance the Church of Rome. The PBS website notes that this documentary "reveals the culture of a Vatican few outsiders have seen, plagued by corruption, cover-ups and ruthless power struggles. . . . 'Unless you spend some time inside this kind of culture, it's very hard to believe that it could be like this,' journalist Robert Mickens tells *Frontline*. How did the Vatican get to this point? Just how far does the corruption extend? Is there hope for meaningful reform?" Parallels here with Westminster's handling of the Shepherd-Gaffin dispute are striking.

Chapter Six

A Denomination Stakes Its Position
The Orthodox Presbyterian Church's Study on Republication[1]

THE REPUBLICATION REPORT OPENS by stating the mandate given to the committee of five members: "The 81st General Assembly, in response to an overture from the Presbytery of the Northwest, elected a study committee 'to examine and give its advice as to whether and in what particular senses the concept of the Mosaic Covenant as a republication of the Adamic Covenant is consistent with the doctrinal system taught in the confessional standards of the Orthodox Presbyterian Church.'" In view of the mandate the committee chose to focus on the teachings of Meredith G. Kline as the means of examining and advising the church on theological issues dividing its membership asunder. The committee notes: "On the one hand it may seem that the mandate of the committee is merely one of confessional exegesis. It certainly involves this, and your committee has taken pains to work with and comment upon every area of the standards that is relevant to the mandate. On the other hand, the committee has also worked on numerous passages of Scripture, especially since the very confession we were tasked to study states quite clearly that 'in all controversies of religion, the church is finally to appeal unto them [i.e., the Scriptures]' (WCF 1.8)."[2]

---

1. Previously published as "Troubler of Israel: Report on Republication by the Orthodox Presbyterian Church Assessing the Teaching of Professor Meredith G. Kline."

2. Northwest Theological Seminary stoked the controversy, only to close its doors in 2016, having failed to garner financial support. The demise of the seminary is in large part due to its aggressive promotion of the Shepherd-Gaffin theology. (The report as

SECTION THREE: DEPARTURE FROM HISTORIC REFORMED FEDERALISM

Background to the Study

The modern-day controversy regarding the interpretation of the Mosaic Covenant (the so-called doctrine of "Republication") has been simmering for over forty years. More exactly, it began in the late 1960s in the womb of Westminster Seminary and the OPC in the thinking of Shepherd's predecessor, systematician John Murray. (Shepherd was chosen by Murray to fill his position on the seminary faculty upon retirement. Prior to Murray's death Shepherd claims to have received Murray's approval of his new thinking on the doctrine of the covenants and justification—approval was sought on Murray's death-bed upon a visit to Scotland.)

Traditional, mainstream Reformed theology has taught—from the time of the Protestant Reformation down to the present day—that the Mosaic Covenant is an administration of the single, ongoing "Covenant of Grace" spanning the entire period of redemptive history (from the Fall to the Consummation). *Peculiar to the Mosaic economy, however, is the operation of the works-inheritance-principle in a very restricted sphere or manner.* A number of explanations have been provided within historic Reformed theology concerning this unique covenantal arrangement in the period extending from Moses to Christ, what is the old economy of redemption. Dissatisfied with this element in Reformed doctrine Murray set out to "recast" the doctrine of the covenants, at the very time that Barthianism was on the ascendency in most Reformed circles in Europe and elsewhere. Murray clearly was not a Barthian, but his novel teaching did imbibe some of the new thinking that was quickly gaining ground. And so it was Murray who opened to door at Westminster to the radical deviation in covenant theology struck by Shepherd and his staunchest supporter, Richard Gaffin Jr., co-author, if not father of the New Theology.

From the broader vantage point of the history of scholastic Reformed orthodoxy, Murray's view gave expression to the theology of English Puritanism, notably, the view that came to dominate in the time after the framing of the *Westminster Standards*. From that point onwards, there were two distinct interpretations of the Mosaic Covenant within international Calvinism, one which acknowledged the works-inheritance principle *as an administrative principle operative within the Mosaic covenant of grace,* the other denying any such *covenantal* operation (both sides did recognize the principle of natural law binding upon all God's image-bearers, human and

---

provided on the OPC website provides no pagination, a major oversight.)

angelic, requiring perfect obedience). The "Puritan" view maintained that the Mosaic Covenant was exclusively a covenant of grace (like the new covenant established by Christ), a covenant lacking the "merit" (or "works") principle as a component of the administration of God's covenant with his elect people. Crucial here, additionally, is recognition of the requisite theological distinction between decretive election to salvation (applicable to all those for whom Christ died) and national, theocratic election (the election of ancient Israel under Moses as covenant-mediator).[3]

Shepherd's dismissal from the faculty of Westminster did not bring closure to the raging dispute. The legacy left by Shepherd, aggressively nurtured by Gaffin who remained on the seminary faculty, became ever more deeply entrenched, despite all efforts to eradicate heterodox teaching from the seminary and the church. In 2004 the 71st General Assembly of the OPC adopted its brief "Statement on Justification," in an effort to address the unresolved debate concerning the foundational doctrine of justification by faith apart from the good works of the believer (faith alone as the "instrument" of justification). The Statement concluded by announcing the erection of a study committee comprising seven members "to critique the teachings of the New Perspective on Paul, Federal Vision, *and other like teachings concerning the doctrine of justification and other related doctrines,* as they are related to the Word of God and our subordinate standards, with a view to giving a clear statement to the presbyteries, sessions and seminaries, and report back to the 72nd GA" (*emphasis mine*). The major study report on justification was presented and received by the 73rd General Assembly in 2006; it was reprinted and posted on the denomination's website in 2007.[4]

---

3. The Puritan-Murray view insists that the Mosaic Covenant, like the new covenant, is a covenant of grace (having no works-inheritance principle in its administration). It therefore follows that the principle enunciated in Leviticus 18:5 ("do this and live") is, in proper covenantal context, at one with the grace-inheritance principle. And looking to the prelapsarian covenant, it is likewise argued that there is no works-inheritance principle, if by that we mean that Adam would earn reward and blessing from God for faithful covenant-keeping (i.e., human "merit"). The ground of inheritance, in this view, is (non-soteric) grace, but grace nevertheless (not "works"). Consistently applied, the result of this thinking dissolves the crucial antithesis between the Covenant of Works and the Covenant of Grace, in terms of the principle of inheritance (reward). Clearly, this is not the intent of the framers of the *Westminster Standards*, despite confusion in theological formulation.

4. The "Report on Justification" provides scant attention to Shepherd's radical (and highly influential) teaching. The report is marred by inadequate discussion of the importance of the doctrine of the Covenant of Works and the law/grace antithesis—the

Section Three: Departure from Historic Reformed Federalism

A decade later, the study report entitled "Report of the Committee to Study Republication" was presented and received at the 83rd General Assembly in 2016. Curiously, the OPC did not move in any official capacity to take up this highly divisive topic among its constituency long before now, waiting instead for the passing of Professor Meredith G. Kline, who had challenged the views of Murray and Shepherd on the doctrine of the covenants as early as the 1960s. (Given his importance in the life of the seminary and the denomination, criticism of Murray has been difficult for many to hear, let alone accept.[5]) Kline held tenaciously to the view of

---

matter of the propriety of the term "grace" applied to the prelasarian covenant pales in comparison. It was reported to me that David VanDrunen and Gaffin, as members of the OPC committee to study justification, were at odds regarding the writing of the report. VanDrunen, who chaired the committee, happily did secure the upper hand. But then again, Gaffin knew that all General Assembly study reports are not binding documents, but rather "food for further thought," *i.e.*, guides to ongoing study within the denomination. See my critique of this report in *Federalism and the Westminster Tradition*, 48–50.

It bears repeating: Though Gaffin served as one of the members of the study committee on justification, it would be a great mistake if one were to infer from this circumstance that Gaffin himself agreed with those aspects of the discussion that impinged upon the views of Shepherd (which, in all essential features, is the same as that held by Gaffin). Three factors must be taken into account: (1) as noted above, the General Assembly reports "do not have the force of constitutional documents, namely, our Confession of Faith and Catechisms and Book of Church Order," and therefore are not binding (Gaffin recognizes that the committee report on justification bears the input of the several members, and all do not necessarily agree *in toto*); (2) despite *private* conversations individuals have had with Gaffin, any comments he has made distancing himself from Shepherd are to be questioned (Gaffin has never made a *public* statement denouncing any of Shepherd's heterodox views—he has never recanted heretical teaching); and (3) Gaffin's active involvement in supporting Shepherd throughout the seminary controversy, leading up to Shepherd's dismissal from the faculty, and his own writings bear witness to the fact Gaffin is the co-author, if not father, of Westminster's deviant teaching on justification and the covenants.

5. Cornelis P. Venema in "The Mosaic Covenant: A 'Republication' of the Covenant of Works? (35–101) complains: "[T. David] Gordon's attack upon John Murray in his chapter seems to exceed the bounds of propriety for an academic essay in biblical theology. For example, he asserts that Murray not only could not have made any sense of Paul's argument in Galatians, but also that whatever he would have written would be 'obfuscatory in the highest degree' (253). And, as if that were not enough, he adds, 'I like to think that he [i.e. Murray] was aware that he was entirely flummoxed by Paul's reasoning, and that he therefore determined not to write anything about the matter until he could make some sense of it.' In actual fact, Murray does address the matter directly in his commentary on the book of Romans, which includes an appendix on Paul's appeal to Leviticus 18:5, that we will consider in what follows. Furthermore, Gordon neglects to note that Murray addresses the interpretation of Galatians 3 in his *Redemption Accomplished and Applied* (44–45), and that his lectures on Galatians at Westminster Theological Seminary are available to the public (see http://sites.google.com/site/themosaiccovenant/

classic Reformed theology; regrettably, his position found little sympathy and support among some faculty colleagues in Philadelphia, those who had exercised the greatest influence on the direction of the seminary and the OPC. The decision finally to form a denominational study committee came after several years of debate and petition to General Assembly.⁶

The 83rd General Assembly ended one day earlier than had been scheduled, and the presentation of the committee report was reserved until the final afternoon of the Assembly, one of the last items to be addressed. Doubtless, it was determined to withhold discussion of the study report on so volatile a subject in order not to distract the Assembly from the other business that was scheduled. (The report was not publicly made available until September 2, 2016, when it was posted on the denominational website.) It was reiterated at the 2016 Assembly that, as in all cases, "General Assembly papers are thoughtful and weighty treatises on important matters but do not have the force of constitutional documents, namely, our Confession of Faith and Catechisms and Book of Church Order" (citation taken from the OPC website and reiterated at the opening of the report on republication). How this study will be received across the denomination and within the broader Reformed community remains to be seen.⁷

To be sure, much interest in this church study has been generated over the years. John Edward Knox, a member of the OPC, writes: "The doctrine

---

john-murray)" (78, note 58). Kline held the conviction that Murray's misconstrual and recasting of Reformed covenant theology was blatantly wrong and inexcusable on his part as Westminster's systematician. "He should have known better," Kline correctly reasoned.

6. Perhaps the OPC will yet produce a history of the Shepherd controversy—including, notably, Gaffin's role and ardent defense of Shepherd from the mid-1970s onwards. Such a history must critique Gaffin's own unorthodox teaching on justification and the covenants which has persisted ever since the days of Shepherd's dismissal from Westminster Seminary in 1982.

7. Apparently, one of the few exceptions in granting others who were not delegates to the 2016 General Assembly early access to the report on republication, Lee Irons (a member of the Presbyterian Church in America) had the opportunity to read in advance the report in the GA minutes. According to Darryl Hart's summary of the GA (http://www.opc.org/nh.html?article_id=895), debate of the report concerned only its dissemination! Discussion "seesawed," according to one internet posting (from Cedar OPC, Hudsonville, MI). Hart's account offers an entirely fallacious and evasive reason for the denominational controversy, what he suggests to be a lack of knowledge concerning differing views over the course of the history of Reformed teaching leading up to the views of Murray and Kline (the two theologians specifically named by Hart). *Rather, the reason was most immediately and directly the teaching of Shepherd and the controversy that ensued.*

of republication was the focal point of one of the reports given at this year's GA, and many people are looking to this report to bring some peace in the Reformed world. Whether or not it will settle things down, history will determine."[8] Likewise, Matthew W. Kingsbury, pastor of Park Hill OPC in Denver, comments: "The most eagerly anticipated item on the docket of the 83rd General Assembly of the OPC was the report of a special committee to study republication."[9]

Summary of the Principle Argument(s) in the Report

There are three parts to the study: (1) a summary of the covenant theology as set forth in the *Westminster Standards*; (2) a consideration of the several views of the doctrine of republication found among Reformed theologians; and (3) the conclusion of the committee ("advice" to the church constituency). The committee is well aware of the voluminous literature on the subject in dispute. It concedes: "No doubt, some of the present disagreements have been occasioned by a resurgence of writings on the doctrine of republication, which have brought a new level of discussion and debate to the church on this matter." Endnote 7 of the report lists many of the works in purview. This, however, is the full extent of "interaction" with the relevant literature. Such points to the lack of competency of the committee assigned to write this study report.[10]

8. John Edward Knox, "Republication: A Pre-OPC GA Defense," *Torrey Gazette*, June 14, 2016, http://torreygazette.com/blog/2016/6/14/republication-a-pre-opc-ga-defense.

9. Matthew W. Kingsbury, "Administrative and Substantial," *The Presbyterian Curmudgeon*, June 13, 2016, http://presbyteriancurmudgeon.blogspot.com/2016/06/administrative-substantial.html. Members of the committee comprised the following: Craig Troxel (chair), Lane Tipton, Bryan Estelle, Chad Van Dixhoorn, and Benjamin Swinburnson. The principle disputants serving on this committee were Estelle (representing the mainstream Reformed view) and Swinburnson (representing the "Puritan" view).

10. Endnote 7 reads as follows: See, for example, the following: Lee Irons, "Redefining Merit," 253–69; Ward, *God and Adam*; White and Beisner, "Covenant, Inheritance, and Typology: Understanding the Principles at Work in God's Covenants," in *By Faith Alone*, 147–70; Estelle, et al., *The Law Is Not of Faith: Essays on Works and Grace in the Mosaic Covenant*; Dennison, et al., "Merit or 'Entitlement' in Reformed Covenant Theology: A Review," 3–152; Ferry, "Works in the Mosaic Covenant: A Reformed Taxonomy." This thesis contains a bibliography at the end. Michael Brown and Zach Keele, *Sacred Bond: Covenant Theology Explored* (Grandville, MI: Reformed Fellowship, 2012); Mark Jones, "In What Sense?" review of *The Law Is Not of Faith, Ordained Servant* 10 (2010): 115–119; Brian Lee, "Reconciling the Two Covenants in the Old Testament," review of *The Law Is Not of Faith, Ordained Servant* 10 (2010):120–26; Cornelis Venema, "The

Since the relationship of the covenant of works to the Mosaic covenant is such a significant part of our mandate, this is one issue that we will address in light of the subject of merit. It seems to the committee that chapter 7 of the WCF permits one to use the language of grace to describe the pre-fall situation; not redemptive grace, but in a more general manner or for other reasons—even as it was commonplace in the seventeenth century to do. Nevertheless, the Westminster Confession does not invoke the category of grace to explain Adam's pre-fall state, but God's voluntary condescension (WCF 7.1). This may be a deliberate choice in light of shifting paradigms of the time. However, it is also permissible to use the language of merit in order to describe the possibility of Adam's obedience in the covenant of works (and perhaps it is even wise this side of Karl Barth, the Federal Vision proponents, and uncritical advocates of the New Perspective on Paul). Seventeenth-century Reformed theologian Johannes Braun did so, as did the Dutch Reformed theologian Salomon Van Til (1643-1713).[11]

Mosaic Covenant: A 'Republication' of the Covenant of Works? A Review Article: *The Law Is Not of Faith: Essays on Works and Grace in the Mosaic Covenant*," *Mid-America Journal of Theology* 21 (2010): 35–102; David VanDrunen, "Israel's Recapitulation of Adam's Probation Under the Law of Moses," *WTJ* 73 (2011): 303–24; Michael Brown, *Christ and the Condition: The Covenant Theology of Samuel Petto (1624-1711)* (Grand Rapids: Reformation Heritage Books, 2012); Brian Lee, "Why I Hold to Republication" *Christian Renewal* (13 Nov 2013): 41–43; Mark A. Collingridge and Brett A. McNeill, *Republication: A Biblical, Confessional and Historical Defense* (Paper submitted to PNW Presbytery, available on PDF). This paper also has a 15 page appendix by David Inks, "What John Calvin Really Said," which is a polemic against Venema's claims; J.V. Fesko (with response by Cornelis Venema), "The Republication of the Covenant of Works," *Confessional Presbyterian* 8 (2012): 197–227; Cornelis Venema (with response by J.V. Fesko), "Sic et Non. Views in Review: II. Westminster Seminary California Distinctives? The Republication of the Covenant of Works," *Confessional Presbyterian* 9 (2013): 157–87; Andrew M. Elam, Robert C. Van Kooten, and Randall A. Bergquist, eds., *Merit and Moses: A Critique of the Klinean Doctrine of Republication* (Eugene, OR: Wipf & Stock, 2014). This is essentially (with only slight modification) the report that was submitted by the authors to the PNW Presbytery as "A Booklet on Merit in the Doctrine of Republication," (April 2013). This contains a bibliography at the end; J. V. Fesko, *The Theology of the Westminster Standards* (Wheaton, IL: Crossway, 2014), especially 138–67; David VanDrunen, *Divine Covenants and Moral Order: A Biblical Theology of Natural Law*, Emory University Studies in Law and Religion, ed. John Witte, Jr. (Grand Rapids: Eerdmans, 2014), especially 282–367; Lee Irons, "Review of *Merit and Moses*" (http://www.upper-register.com/papers/response-to-merit-and-moses.pdf).

11. The same point can be found in Murray's formulation of the "Adamic administration" (what in biblical theology is the original covenant of works established by God with Adam at creation).

Section Three: Departure from Historic Reformed Federalism

The committee understands that "Both parties [those who affirm and those who deny the works-principle in the Mosaic Covenant] can affirm WCF 7.1 wholeheartedly (on the issue of grace or merit before the fall). There is room for further reflection and dialogue on this point over which hearty and brotherly discourse may occur." *This admission calls into question the need to raise the question regarding use of the term "merit" altogether. It does not get to the heart of the controversy.* (For years, Gaffin has used this issue to obscure and confound the issues in dispute—a ploy in the hands of the chief miscreant.[12])

This brings us to Part One ("The Westminster Standards and Covenant Theology"). Here the report takes up the important Creator/creature distinction, what is "foundational to all covenant theology." However, the report questions: "How can there be fellowship or any covenant relationship between man and his Creator except by God's 'voluntary condescension' to him (WCF 7.1)?" The answer given: "He must descend to us; we cannot ascend to him. Thus, it is God who entered into a "covenant of life" with our race, and this through a "special act of providence" (WCF 4.2; LC 17,20; SC 12)." Appealing to the Standards, rather than to Scripture, the report insists that God's covenant with Adam at the beginning was an addition to the prior state of nature. This nature/covenant dichotomy is unbiblical; it is simply wrong.[13] The report then moves to consider the significant role of

---

12. As argued in my previous book, *Gospel Grace*, the attempt on the part of Shepherd and Gaffin to exploit the speculative, scholastic nature/covenant dichotomy frequently employed in Reformed dogmatics for the purpose of dissolving the law/gospel antithesis is wholly destructive of the orthodox doctrine of justification by faith (alone) and the doctrine of the original Covenant of Works, the covenant established by God with Adam as federal head of humankind. The Report on Justification failed to advance biblical understanding of the controverted issues lying at the heart of the dispute, this serving only to perpetuate former error in the scholastic understanding of the Covenant of Works (wherein it is erroneously held that grace is the basis of the reward for faithful covenant-keeping). Such a view undermines the merit-principle of inheritance, that which stands in contrast to the grace-principle of inheritance in the Covenant of Grace. To dispel misunderstanding and confusion in the minds of so many today, what is clearly demanded is a reformulation of doctrine that faithfully conveys the teaching of Scripture. *The term "grace" pertains exclusively to God's redemptive provision for fallen humanity.*

13. Later the report maintains again: "while our first parents bore this image and were embedded with this law, the distance between God and humanity is so great that God voluntary condescended to us, without which we would have no benefit from him at all. God's act of 'voluntary condescension' was to establish a covenant (WCF 7.1). In other words, the law of God was implanted in us at creation, and yet we cannot flourish without covenant, and so God brought our first parents into a covenantal relationship with himself through a 'special act of providence' (SC 12). This means, among other

typology in the interpretation of the Mosaic economy, that in relation to the new covenant. "An important, but indirect way of addressing the question [of republication] is to consider how our confession views typology, for those who hold to a republication of the covenant of works in some sense tend to see a more expansive than limited understanding of typology in the Mosaic economy." Though the discussion here is of limited help, in our judgment, at least there is a recognition of its importance.

With a view to the confessional teaching concerning the principle of natural law, as that pertains to the original covenant order and to the Mosaic dispensation, the report notes: "Perhaps a door is cracked open but nothing enters the rest of the confession to support the systematic development of any substantial republication of the covenant of works or a works principle [in the Mosaic economy]. No such principle is ever granted any typological importance in our confessional standards. Nor is the Mosaic economy bracketed off in the confession, or even offered a unique place within the Old Testament—indeed, the whole Old Testament is simply characterized as 'the time of the law' (WCF 7.5)." This omission (or rather silence) in the *Confession* simply underscores the need within the Reformed theological tradition for further elucidation (the seventeenth-century *Confession* does not have the last word, contrary to the opinion of the committee).

The study returns once again to the issue of "merit" in the description of the covenant-of-works feature operative in both the Adamic and Mosaic administrations. "One important subject raised in some discussions about republication is the relationship between a work and a reward. Is it the case that there is some necessary correspondence between a work and its reward? Or is a connection between the two a matter which God himself can freely determine as he pleases, but once determined, is obliged, in faithfulness to his own word, to maintain? In terms of classical theology and philosophy, is the relationship between works and rewards real or nominal (the latter being a position sometimes called 'simple justice', '*ex*

---

things, that creation does not seem to be synonymous with covenant." And again, in different terms the report states: "it appears, then, that the implantation of the moral law in the human conscience is coincident with creation, and yet the creation of a covenant falls under the realm of providence. In other words, from the viewpoint of the confession, this law on their hearts was not naked; it was clothed from (almost?) the beginning in a covenantal arrangement. It is for that reason the man and the woman were not alone together in the garden; it is in that way they were enabled to live in relationship with God. Natural law does not seem to be synonymous with the covenant of works."

pacto merit,' or 'covenantal justice')?" Here again the discussion is confusing and unhelpful, serving only to cloud the issues in dispute.[14]

We now come to Part Two ("Views on Republication"), the longest section of the report. Recall that the formulation of Kline has been chosen by the committee to be the focus of ongoing controversy within church and seminary (this was determined by the committee, not the General Assembly mandate). The report identifies four distinct viewpoints (as follows):

> View 1: The Mosaic covenant is in substance a covenant of works, promising eternal life and/or salvation upon condition of perfect, personal, and perpetual obedience.
>
> View 2: The Mosaic covenant is in substance a mixed covenant, containing elements of both a covenant of works and a covenant of grace.
>
> View 3: The Mosaic covenant in substance is a subservient covenant, promising temporal life in Canaan upon condition of perfect obedience to the moral, ceremonial, and judicial laws.
>
> View 4: The Mosaic covenant is in substance a covenant of grace, although uniquely administered in a manner appropriate to the situation of God's people at that time.

It is my contention that Kline's formulation does embody many elements found within the Reformed theological tradition from the sixteenth and seventeenth centuries onward. None of the views in the report is an accurate

---

14. Mention of the "ontological" difference between the "one righteous act" of the First and Second Adams is wholly irrelevant. Hence, the report mistakenly concludes: "not only is there a 'great disproportion' between the works of the redeemed 'and the glory to come,' but also an 'infinite distance that is between us and God' (WCF 16.5). Even pre-fall merit is thus excluded, in any proportional sense, because of the ontological difference between the Creator and the creature. Adam had a capacity for perfect, personal, and perpetual obedience, but the value of that obedience was far less than the promised reward. Quite apart from the problem of sin (also discussed in 16.5), it seems, there was no possibility of Adam or his descendants accelerating an eschatological or glorified state by means of any real merit of his own; he could only do so through a covenantal arrangement, where God, in his benevolent freedom, would reward his obedience with a gift beyond that which he had earned." *The members of the Committee simply do not grasp the importance and significance of the law/gospel antithesis, the opposition between reward received as a matter of redemptive grace (i.e., salvation in Christ) and reward based upon covenantal obedience (the eschatological blessing proffered to Adam in the original Covenant of Works for obedience to God the Lord). Crucial here in the discussion, additionally, is the related doctrine of imputation, including the representative headship of the Two Adams, something largely neglected in the report.*

description of the Kline-Karlberg interpretation, what is demanded in this study, as defined by the committee.[15] The closest is the fourth view in its taxonomy. According to the report, "Positions one and four represent opposite poles of the spectrum: from no grace to pure grace. Positions two and three represent attempts to mitigate this polarity. The mixed covenant view does this by combining works and grace as equally ultimate aspects of the essence of the Mosaic covenant. The subservient covenant does this by temporalizing the works element, restricting the relationship of works to blessings on the earthly realm only, thus mitigating the tension with works and grace at the level of eternal salvation." In my judgment, the committee's taxonomy is not a

---

15. Alongside Professor Kline, I had the unique privilege of crystalizing Reformed interpretation of the covenants over the course of seven years of study at Westminster—three for the master of divinity, one for the masters in theology (New Testament studies), and three for the doctorate in theology (Reformation/Post-Reformation studies), leading up to the writing of my dissertation, entitled "The Mosaic Covenant and the Concept of Works in Reformed Hermeneutics: A historical-critical analysis with special attention to early covenant eschatology" (ThD dissertation, Westminster Theological Seminary, 1980), available at University Microfilms International (Ann Arbor, MI and London, England: #8024938). Kline was appointed as one of the dissertation readers by virtue of his expertise and interest in ongoing discussions within the faculty that had transpired since the mid-1970s. My master's thesis is entitled "Law in Pauline Eschatology: The Historical Qualification of Justification by Faith" (Th.M. thesis, Westminster Theological Seminary, 1977). On the cover of Kline's magnum opus I wrote: "In *Kingdom Prologue* Meredith G. Kline, foremost OT scholar and theologian at the turn of this century, weaves together in biblical-theological fashion various and complex aspects of Old Testament life and worship, preeminently in terms of the biblical concepts of kingdom and covenant. Building on the tradition of (old) Princeton theologian Geerhardus Vos, the author takes Biblical Theology to new heights in the history of Reformed interpretation of the Old and New Testaments. In the pages of this book, Kline explains to his readers the place and importance of the first book of Moses, the Book of Genesis, in the overall structure and theology of the divine covenants from the creation of the world to its consummation. At the same time Kline's theological analysis effectively draws out the missionary and apologetic implications of the biblical text, and in so doing clarifies the unique role and mission of the Church in the world. I warmly and enthusiastically commend this work, Kline's *magnum opus,* to the serious student of the Bible."

Compare D. Patrick Ramsey, "In Defense of Moses" (373–400); and Brenton C. Ferry, "Cross-Examining Moses' Defense" (163–68). Venema remarks: "Karlberg's interpretation of the history of Reformed covenant theology suffers from an undue attachment to the formulations of Meredith Kline. It is noteworthy that the authors of *The Law is Not of Faith* do not refer to the fine study of my colleague, J. Mark Beach, *Christ and the Covenant*" ("The Mosaic Covenant," 42, note 8). See my critique of Beach's study in my book *Engaging Westminster Calvinism*—Chapter Three: "Recovering the Mosaic Covenant as Law and Gospel." Beach has yet to respond to my criticism(s) of his formulation.

Section Three: Departure from Historic Reformed Federalism

fair representation of the Reformed covenantal tradition. No less confusing is the following summary description of the four views (as follows):

1. The first view states that the substance of the Adamic covenant is republished to Israel pure and simple. God makes a covenant with Israel requiring perfect, personal obedience and promises eternal life upon condition of such obedience.

2. The second view states that the substance of the covenant is *in part* a republication of the Adamic covenant of works pure and simple.

3. The third views states that the substance of the covenant is a republication of the Adamic covenant of works, although adjusted to temporal blessings in Canaan.

4. The fourth view argues that the substance of the Sinaitic covenant is in substance *not* a republication of the Adamic covenant of works, but instead an administration of the unfolding covenant of grace. Any republication or restatement of the covenant of works appears solely on the administrative level, and in a way that is consistent with its fundamentally gracious substance.

The complexities involved with the interpretation of the Mosaic Covenant in Reformed theology—and Protestant evangelical theology more widely—have always been recognized. The Kline-Karlberg formulation has been offered to the Reformed academy as providing the most satisfying formulation of Scripture, building squarely upon historic Reformed teaching. The report speaks of "two interpretations of Kline's view." The question for the committee is this: What is the proper interpretation of Kline's covenant theology? Juggling two readings of Kline only adds to the tediousness of this report. Looking more closely at the failure of the committee to read Kline aright we are obliged to give account to some degree of development in Kline's own thinking (and here is where Kline and I collaborated in reformulating the Reformed doctrine of the covenants in order to bring out the best in our theological tradition). The report correctly notes:

> In *By Oath Consigned*, one of Kline's early books, he utilizes a distinction between the Mosaic order and the Sinaitic covenant itself. He affirms that the "old Mosaic order" as a whole is an administration of the covenant of grace. Nonetheless, he speaks of the Sinaitic covenant itself as a "specific legal whole," identifying it as making the inheritance "to be by law, not by promise—not by faith but by works." In this context he speaks of the "difference" between this

Sinaitic covenant and the covenant of grace as "radical." He also refers to Paul's "radical assessment of the *nature* of the Sinaitic Covenant as something opposite to promise and faith." Kline further states that in this way the "Sinaitic Covenant" can be viewed "as a separate entity with a character of its own." These statements directly address the nature or substance of the Sinai covenant in itself. Taken together, they suggest that Kline does view the Sinaitic covenant as a separate covenant, distinct in nature from the covenant of grace.

The fact is this: Kline modified his position in the late 1970s. The faculty of Westminster was fully aware of this change. Kline rightly faulted Palmer Robertson for deliberately ignoring Kline's reformulation in his book of covenant theology.[16] Inexplicably, the report contends:

> Kline's later works maintain similar emphases when describing the nature of the Sinai covenant. In *Kingdom Prologue*, Kline argues that the "typal kingdom of the old covenant" was a covenant "governed by the works principle." In this "Israel as the theocratic nation was mankind stationed once again in a paradise-sanctuary, under probation in a covenant of works." Relative to their probationary experience as a theocratic nation in the land, Israel was under a covenant of works opposite in nature to a covenant of grace. In *God, Heaven and Har Magedon* (Kline's last work), this same theme is highlighted. There he argues that in the Mosaic era, God superimposes over the Abrahamic covenant "a works arrangement, the Torah covenant with its 'do this and live' principle (cf. Lev. 18:5), the opposite of the grace-faith principle (Gal. 3–4; Rom. 10:5, 6)." Later in the work he explicitly identifies this as the "Sinaitic covenant of works" and the "Torah covenant of works." Significantly, this works principle did not apply to "individual, eternal salvation" but "was rather the governing principle in the typological sphere." Nonetheless, these lines of argument focus on the nature of the Sinai covenant itself, which Kline's later writings consistently identify as being a works covenant in contrast to a covenant of grace. The Kline-Karlberg position insists that the Mosaic Covenant is an administration of the single, ongoing Covenant of Grace spanning the entire redemptive epoch (from the Fall to the Consummation). At the same time, the Mosaic Covenant is a parenthesis in the history of redemption, in that the principle of works-inheritance (antithetical to faith-inheritance)

---

16. See O. Palmer Robertson's *Christ of the Covenants*.

functions in the typological sphere, and is regulative of temporal life in the land of Canaan.[17]

We now come to that section of the report that attempts to distill Kline's theology of circumcision and baptism. According to Kline, the initiatory signs of the redemptive covenant, *sacramentally speaking*, convey blessing to the elect and curse to the non-elect. Consistent with the teaching of historic Reformed theology, Kline maintains that redemptive covenant is broader than election. That is to say, the *proper purpose* of redemptive covenant is salvation in Christ. But the administration of God's covenant in the life of the church as the community of faith, across the old and new economies of redemption, is broader than securing the salvation of all those elected in Christ. The historical administration of redemptive covenant includes the non-elect, who for one reason or another are numbered among the people of God (and so this circumstance will persist until the return of Christ and the final separation of the wheat from the tares on the Day of Judgment). None of this teaching in Kline's work is brought to the reader's attention in the report. But it is only from this standpoint that one can make sense of what the report explains in Kline's writings when it states:

> Kline believes that apostasy is possible under the covenant of grace. Such a belief coheres with a theology admitting to dual sanctions of blessing or curse appended to the sacraments of circumcision/

---

17. The committee concludes its evaluation of Kline's view in the following words: "The four strands of teaching adduced for this interpretation of Kline indicate to many readers that he teaches a form of substantial republication. Kline himself freely speaks of the complex relation between works and grace within the Mosaic economy. He does not deny that grace is present in the Mosaic period, nor the fact that grace underlies the Sinai covenant of works probation. He also restricts the works principle to the temporal kingdom of Canaan, and rejects the idea that there was a different way of salvation under the Mosaic era. Nonetheless this does not remove the fact that on this interpretation the Sinai covenant itself is substantially and by nature governed by a basic principle that is decidedly not gracious. It distinctively reflects the substantial principles of a covenant-of-works probation in contrast to a covenant of grace. In these paragraphs, then, and in others like them, Kline maintains that the Mosaic economy contains a distinct covenant that is itself a covenant of works in contrast to the covenant of grace. It is for that reason that Kline's teaching on the Mosaic covenant and the covenant of works can be categorized as a form of substantial republication.... The works surveyed in the report below span the range of Kline's publishing career, from his earlier work in *Treaty of the Great King* (1963) to his final published book, *God, Heaven and Har Magedon* (2006). A guide for understanding Kline, borne out by a careful reading of his entire corpus, is that his biblical theology of the covenant of grace does not undergo any substantial alteration. Rather, from his earliest works up until his final work, a basic point of continuity emerges."

> baptism. Those under the Lordship of God in the covenant of grace face a judgment according to works if they fail to walk by faith in the Messiah, who bears judgment for them. Kline says, "Moreover, the newness of the New Covenant does not consist in a reduction of the Covenant of Redemption to the principle of election and guaranteed blessing. Its law character is seen in this too that it continues to be a covenant with dual sanctions . . . having, in particular, anathemas to pronounce and excommunications to execute."

Kline's theology of the sacraments becomes a critical focusing lens by which we can distinguish and relate corporate and individual apostasy and gain greater clarity on the nature of the Mosaic covenant, Israel's national obedience, and the typico-symbolic recapitulation of Adam's sin and exile in Israel's protracted apostasy.

One of the reasons for the legal function of the Mosaic law—Israel's "tutor" or "schoolmaster"—is the fact that Israel's tenure in the promised land of Canaan is contingent upon Israel's *own* obedience to covenantal law, not the substitutionary obedience of Christ imputed to all those united to him by grace through faith. If the basis of life in Canaan was soteric grace, then the reward (life and prosperity in Canaan) would be unlosable. The report correctly observes:

> What this requires us to appreciate in Kline's thought is the distinction between the way Christ's obedience secures the eschatological kingdom in opposition to the way that Israel's disobedience forfeits the typal kingdom. Kline's point is that Israel's situation correlates itself to the fallen Adamic order in the way that disobedience forfeits inheritance—a scenario that stands in the starkest contrast to the way that Christ's obedience merits the eschatological inheritance. Therefore, while the grace of Christ's suretyship underwrites and enables Israel's obedience at the level of the *ordo salutis*, his obedience does not secure the everlasting maintenance of the typal kingdom at the level of the *historia salutis*. If his suretyship did secure the typal kingdom perpetually, that order would endure forever. The typal kingdom order did not endure forever, because its permanent maintenance was not rooted in the suretyship of Christ but the obedience of national Israel. This is perhaps the core insight of Kline's theology of the works principle.

At long last, we come to the committee's summary and conclusion regarding Kline's view of republication. The road here has been long and tedious. In summation, the report states:

Section Three: Departure from Historic Reformed Federalism

> Kline's viewpoint is perhaps best described as an administrative re-enactment within national Israel of the outcome of the covenant of works with Adam, adjusted to the realities of sin, grace and redemptive typology, resulting in exile from the inheritance-land of Canaan. While other interpretations of Kline would suggest he endorses substantial republication of the covenant of works with Adam, the line of argument developed in this chapter, particularly the integral role played by Abraham as the redemptive-historical frame of reference for the nature of corporate Israel's obedience, suggests otherwise. As for alleged weaknesses in Kline's formulation of covenant theology, the committee believes "his use of 'merit' language is 'unfortunate' in light of the history of the Reformed tradition, although it maintains that the substance of his views are orthodox. Even if Kline's proposal on this reading is orthodox and coheres with the system of truth outlined in the standards, there are still areas that need further clarification and refinement."

At the same time, legitimate questions can continue to be raised regarding the usefulness of these qualifications as applied to the term merit. Kline's qualifications, as understood within this interpretive paradigm, are sufficient to stave off the charge of heterodoxy. Nonetheless, some could think that the qualifications are useful in themselves, but that they lose utility insofar as they apply to a nuanced view of typological merit in distinction from *ex pacto* merit. Thus, the question remains whether or not it might be desirable to find language other than typological merit to express the same concepts Kline expressed, and this question ought to provide the context for continued intramural discussion within our denomination.[18]

Finally, we arrive at the recommendations and advice of the committee in Part Three (the briefest section in the report). The governing principle in God's covenant with humankind, pre-and post-Fall, is grace, either non-redemptive grace or soteric grace—but grace all the same. The report asserts:

> our standards affirm that the merit of Christ, the God-man and mediator, consists in his perfect, personal, proportional, profitable, and free obedience. Christ offers his covenant-obedience and sufferings as the representative head of the elect. He thereby fulfills the requirements and removes the penalty of the original covenant of works. Precisely because fallen man cannot fulfill

---

18. Once again, the report falsely reduces the controversy merely to "intramural" debate, and in its judgment deems the tendency in the interpretations of both Shepherd and Kline as moving towards heterodoxy!

these conditions, he is unable (properly speaking) to merit a reward from God of any kind.

This is the very argument that Gaffin has been maintaining since the beginning of the theological controversy in the 1970s. And it has been Gaffin's insistence that Kline's views not be taught at Westminster (Philadelphia); likewise, Kline's teaching is not welcome in the OPC. Gaffin's position has been honored in this Report on Republication. *The jury is in—Professor Meredith G. Kline, the troubler of Israel, is out!*

Karlberg on Kline: A Closing Evaluation

Historically, the two dominant Reformed views on the Mosaic Covenant—that best represented in the OPC context by the divergent thinking of Murray and Kline—have been around for a very long time. What has ignited the bitter dispute within the Westminster Seminary community and beyond, here at the close of the 20th century, well into the 21st? The clear, indisputable answer is the Shepherd-Gaffin theology. At this historical juncture, if Gaffin's teaching is in line with traditional Reformed covenant theology (as widely, but erroneously, alleged), why the raging dispute over the law-works principle operative within the Mosaic Covenant? What accounts for this theological crisis in present-day Calvinism?[19]

19. Biblical theology in the tradition of Geerhardus Vos is precursor to the modern-day Reformed doctrine of republication. In the "Introduction" the authors of *The Law is Not of Faith* reason: "With such rhetoric [urging the "recasting" of covenant theology] Murray released the clutch, and those who had studied under him or were influenced by his writings without appropriate reflection and criticism in these areas set in motion a chain of events that would produce deleterious injuries for confessional Reformed theology and beyond. Norman Shepherd, professor of systematic theology at Westminster Theological Seminary from 1963 to 1982, is a case in point. In his recent book, he too showed great antipathy to any construal of republication in the Mosaic covenant and a works principle represented in such an important passage as Leviticus 18:5, for example" (17). Leading up to the 83rd General Assembly I posted the following three updates: (1) "Republication: A Doctrinal Controversy Four Decades in the Making," posted on *The Aquila Report*, September 4, 2014 [http://theaquilareport.com/republication-a-doctrinal-controversy-four-decades-in-the-making/]; (2) "Addendum to the Republication Controversy," posted on *The Aquila Report*, October 4, 2014 [http://theaquilareport.com/addendum-to-the-republication-controversy/]; and (3) "Current Study on Republication: Where matters presently stand," posted on *Trinity Foundation,* November 2015 [http://www.trinityfoundation.org/update.php?id=2]. In the last posting I made the statement: "Complicating matters, however, the Standards relate the Mosaic law to the original law of nature (what is yet another reference to the principle

Section Three: Departure from Historic Reformed Federalism

Pivotal to the long-standing controversy over the doctrine of justification and the covenants is not Kline's formulation, but rather Murray's mutation ("recasting") of traditional covenant theology and, more immediately, Shepherd's unorthodox deformation of Reformed federalist teaching. The report's "Glossary" contains the name of only one theologian, Meredith Kline, the troubler of Israel. To place Kline's work at the centerpiece of its analysis of the long-standing controversy is a wholly misconceived attempt on the part of the committee members to portray Kline as the leading adversary, the central theological figure and cause of dissension. The report is best read as the denominational tribunal on the orthodoxy of Kline's covenant theology.[20]

---

of works-inheritance). *Reformed theologians uniformly taught that the Mosaic Covenant contained a reiteration of the law of nature (hence the universal, binding character of the Ten Commandments upon all peoples).* A consistent, mature formulation of the theology of the covenants would require many decades of debate and discussion—what is still ongoing within the church and the academy."

The authors of "Merit or 'Entitlement'" in Reformed Covenant Theology" note: "Richard B. Gaffin Jr. has also raised some concerns about the 'republication thesis.' In a recent review of Michael Horton's *Covenant and Salvation*, Gaffin expressed his concern regarding Horton's view that under the Mosaic economy the judicial role of the law in the life of God's people functioned, at the typological level, for inheritance by works (as the covenant of works reintroduced) in antithesis to grace (29). Furthermore, Gaffin sees this position as creating 'an uneasy tension, if not polarization, in the lives of his people between grace/faith and (good) works obedience (*ordo salutis*), especially under the Mosaic economy' (30). Gaffin's comments do not directly address the relationship of Horton's views to the Westminster Confession and the Reformed tradition in general, but they do express his general concern regarding not only the internal consistency of the position, but also how it may detract from an accurate reading of the Old Testament" (25). They conclude: "To our knowledge, Gaffin has also extensively critiqued constructions of the Mosaic covenant as embodying a meritorious works-principle in both his classroom lectures and various public presentations on the doctrine of the covenant. The classroom lectures can be accessed online at www.wts.edu" (25, note 31). The authors are James T. Dennison, Jr., Scott F. Sanborn, and Benjamin W. Swinburnson. In "Current Study on Republication" I noted: "*Kerux*, at present an online *journal* of biblical theology published by Northwest Theological Seminary, had previously published Kline's excellent and insightful studies in the book of Zachariah (since published as *Glory in Our Midst*, 2001). Now the journal has taken a decidedly anti-Klinian stance, this after mounting criticism of the Shepherd-Gaffin 'biblical theology' (which Northwest Seminary heartily commends)."

20. It is curious to read the committee's report concerning the origin and development of this long-standing, disruptive controversy. Gregory Reynolds (Ordained Servant Online, August / September 2012 / Issue: Biblical Theology) remarks: "Meredith G. Kline's theology is sometimes controversial in our church," and that "on several areas of concern." Again, a reversal of the true state of affairs in the OPC. Clair Davis, writing to

A Denomination Stakes Its Position

The Report is unnecessarily tedious, yielding only more confusion in the mind of the reader. What it does indicate is the frustration and the lack of competence on the part of the committee members assigned the task of writing the report. The report does a thoroughgoing disservice to the Reformed church and academy, resulting in a distortion of Kline's theology. Barely a word is made denouncing the heterodox views of Shepherd. Lack of interaction with the extensive literature on the subject under review is without justification, but does serve of purpose of the committee which sees the dispute over doctrine as an purely "intramural" affair. There are only three references to Shepherd's teaching, none of which identify his controversial teaching as heretical; only one indirect reference to Karlberg's writings on this subject and his critical assessment of Westminster Seminary.[21]

Kline regarded me as his "theological son"—it is reasonable that I should take the time to redress the issues raised in the report about Kline's covenant theology and, in so doing, clear the air regarding his position and challenge/correct the widespread misreading and distortion of his work. Who is better poised to clarify matters? If advocates of traditional Reformed covenant theology hold true to their convictions, this report will not sit well; it will only generate more dissension and upheaval. *Within the*

Tom Juodaitis (Trinity Foundation), laments having lost contact with Karlberg (email of March 26, 2015). Perhaps open dialogue would have saved the committee from blatant misreading of Kline's writings.

21. In the paper prepared for the OPC Presbytery of the Northwest, "Republication: A Biblical, Confessional, and Historical Defense," by Mark A. Collingridge and Brett A. McNeill, we read these comments:

> Fathers and brothers, from one perspective, we are happy to write this paper in order to speak about the proper place of the doctrine of republication in historic, confessional Presbyterian and Reformed theology. We stand downstream of a glorious work of our God in the Protestant Reformation wherein the great *solas* of our faith were set forth as never before. Republication is an aspect of that crystallization intended to guard, uphold, and undergird such important doctrines as the law-fulfilling work of our Lord Jesus Christ in His active and passive obedience, justification by faith alone, and the liberty and freedom we enjoy as the sons of God in the new covenant Christ ratified in His blood. We are thankful for the opportunity to do our best to address questions, concerns, and confusions regarding this historic doctrine.
>
> On the other hand, it grieves us that this paper is written under a cloud of accusations, suspicion, contention, and fear. This is never a helpful context for good, edifying, and helpful theological dialogue among brothers and sisters in Christ. Our hope is that, whether or not one agrees with this Reformed insight, these unfortunate storm clouds will dissipate and allow the light of temperance, trust, understanding, and love to shine brightly as is fitting those united to Jesus Christ and bound in our common calling to serve the church. [iv]

SECTION THREE: DEPARTURE FROM HISTORIC REFORMED FEDERALISM

OPC the root of the confusion and the deliberate, calculated diversion away from the Shepherd teaching to that of Kline as regards the Reformed doctrine of the Mosaic Covenant is the crucial law-gospel antithesis.[22] The reason for this is the unwillingness to address elements of the Shepherd formulation which continue to impact teaching in the seminaries and churches, largely the result of Gaffin's dominance. Will Westminster Seminary California follow Estelle and retreat from the doctrine of republication as formulated by Kline (as suggested by this report)? Much remains to be seen.[23]

22. Robertson's history of the dispute, *The Currrent Justification Controversy*, was published by Trinity Foundation long after being suppressed by prevailing powers in the PCA and the OPC. Robertson's account, appearing in 2003, made necessary the OPC "Statement on Justification" (2004) to give the false appearance that the denomination stood squarely within the bounds of Reformed orthodoxy. Included in Robertson's account is Gaffin's role in support of Shepherd. The official Westminster document providing justification for the dismissal of Shepherd from the faculty (establishing the "legal" ground for dismissal of a tenured professor) is entitled "Reason and Specifications Supporting the Action of the Board of Trustees in Removing Professor Shepherd." The committee charged with the task of writing this paper had requested a paper from me critiquing Shepherd's theology, which was provided. The "Reason and Specifications" is available in John W. Robbins, *A Companion to the Current Justification Controversy*, and in other places.

23. W. Robert Godfrey and D. G. Hart explain: "Westminster California was born in the heat of the Shepherd controversy and initially left the Shepherd problem to WTS (especially since Frame tended to defend Shepherd while Strimple and Godfrey had sharply criticized him.) But even with the dismissal of Shepherd in 1981, the issue of the doctrine of justification did not disappear. Some in the Reformed churches continued to defend Shepherd, others embraced the New Perspective on Paul and still others adopted the Federal Vision" (*Westminster Seminary California*, 109).

In a letter to Will Barker (then Dean of the faculty at WTS) Kline wrote: "Mark Karlberg's misgivings concerning the current theological picture at WTS/P are justified" (8/31/94). Kline added: "In my judgment, if the present tendencies are not reversed, perceptive church historians of the future will record that the erosion of Reformational theology (with respect to both the formal and material principles) that began at WTS/P in the seventies of the 20th century continued unchecked into the 21st century." Over the years, R. C. Sproul (Sr.) has been very supportive and encouraging with regard to my critiques of Westminster and all those espousing the New Theology. (One still hopes that Sproul will yet come to realize the impropriety and inappropriateness of applying the biblical-theological term "grace" to the covenant of works, wherein the works-inheritance principle, antithetical to the faith-grace principle, is operative.)

Strimple encouraged me to pursue my doctoral study at WTS. Shepherd was appointed as my doctoral advisor; followed by W. Robert Godfrey when Shepherd requested to step down from that role (Godfrey is currently President of WSC). My years at WTS provided the impetus for renewed discussions of covenant theology, and led to the invitation to bring Kline back to teach on a part-time basis. Clowney had been abroad on sabbatical and would have opposed my admittance into the doctoral program (at a time when the Shepherd controversy had consumed the administration and faculty); it was at this same

From its inception, the OPC had the opportunity to realize the best in Reformed theology, ministry and mission. Of course, no denomination is perfect. As it turns out, the OPC is a failed experiment in American Presbyterianism. Pride and failure to hear and act upon *valid* criticism offered by others sympathetic to the Reformed cause has led to her downfall. What the report on republication proves is that the OPC is incapable of correction and truth-telling. She remains resolute in her refusal to repent of error and deceit. Most notably with respect to the controversy over justification and the covenants, the OPC sees herself as above reproach. Upon the dismissal of Shepherd from Westminster, Robert Strimple decided to turn a blind eye to Gaffin's formulations, not wanting another agonizing round of controversy and ecclesiastical disruption to impede the work and witness of Westminster. The OPC study report on republication is the product of Westminster Seminary (East and West), as evident in the selection of committee members. With regard to the California faculty, Kline was not persuaded that it was taking a clear, decisive stand against the deviant teaching propounded by Gaffin, who has remained steadfast in his support for Shepherd (the same can be said of John Frame).[24]

---

time that Kuschke filed charges against Shepherd in the Philadelphia Presbytery of the OPC. At the very beginning Shepherd requested to serve as my doctoral advisor (each had respect and esteem for one another); in the end Clowney reversed his position and achieved winning Shepherd's dismissal (this after studying my doctoral work, notably as summarized in the 1980 fall issue of *WTJ*). These were unsettling times for so many.

Lee Irons, in his "Response to *Merit and Moses*: A Critique of the Klinean Doctrine of Republication" (http://www.upper-register.com/papers/response-to-merit-and-moses.pdf), rightly laments: "with the publication of *Merit and Moses* and the formation of the OPC Republication Study Committee, it seems their charges are beginning to get some traction. They have even managed to get respected Reformed professors, such as Robert Strimple (another former professor of mine at WSC), Cornelis Venema, and Richard Gaffin, to endorse their book attacking Kline and those of us who appreciate Kline's biblical-theological and covenantal insights. They also were able to get OPC pastor William Shishko to write the Foreword for their book, as well as an endorsement from Presbyterian Church in America (PCA) pastor Mark Jones, author of a recent book on antinomianism. Seeing so many take this book seriously is troubling" (2). Unfortunately, Lee Irons minimizes the error of Shepherd's staunchest defender, Richard Gaffin. As I have pointed out repeatedly, the current dispute in the OPC and in the seminary relates to the contrary views of Kline and Gaffin. For a perceptive analysis of Iron's shortcoming in this very regard, see Stephen M. Cunha, "The Critical Ingredient Missing from Richard B. Gaffin Jr.'s Soteriology," posted on the Trinity Foundation (November 2015): http://www.trinityfoundation.org/update.php?id=3.

24. All of this has been documented in other places. Numerous times in conversation and personal correspondence Kline has asserted Gaffin's denial of the law/gospel antithesis. After engaging Frame on the California campus, Kline found it necessary "to sound

Section Three: Departure from Historic Reformed Federalism

It was never Kline's intent that his work should be the center of controversy. The fact that it came to be so is more a sign of the times, a very sad development for Reformed orthodoxy indeed. Whether we consider Kline's opposition to Gregory Bahnsen's theonomy, the Shepherd-Gaffin reformulation of doctrine (specifically, justification by faith alone, election, and the twofold covenants), or John Murray's recasting of covenant theology, Kline surely is to be recognized and honored for his unwavering stand for the truth of Scripture, for his life-long devotion to the Church of Christ, and for his commitment to orthodox Reformed teaching. The differences between Kline and Murray (notably, interpretation of the Mosaic Covenant) moved to the forefront only as a consequence of the dispute surrounding the teaching of Norman Shepherd.[25] *In a word, the "Report of the Committee to*

---

the alarm against the Shepherd-Gaffin theology more loudly and pointedly than ever" in the classroom and beyond (letter of 3/15/98). With reference to Westminster Theological Seminary in Philadelphia, Kline spoke of "the real nature of that school's vaunted new theologizing program," urging Strimple to insure the clear separation of Westminster Seminary California from WTS. All parties closest to the seminary dispute knew that Kline and I shared the same assessment of Gaffin's role in the formulation and defense of Shepherd's teaching. There was no doubt or reservation on the part of either one of us. With respect to our mutual devotion to the Reformed faith and its covenantal exposition, Kline regarded me his "son," his theological heir. To be sure, I have been the leading critic of Frame's multi-perspectivalism, as well as the leading critic of Gaffin's own unorthodox formulations of the issues in dispute (as their responses indicate, both Gaffin and Frame have been very much aware of this circumstance). In some quarters, I also have been falsely labeled "controversial"—a reversal of the true state of affairs! Several efforts and devious tactics have been employed in the attempt to silence me.

Dennison, Sanborn and Swinburnson state: "In fairness to Fesko and Ferry, we are encouraged that they have recognized many of the historical-theological errors in Karlberg's analysis (78–79)—one that has played a large role in shaping many Klineans' understanding of the Reformed tradition. Still, they do not seem to be as forthright as they might have been about the source of many of these basic errors, namely, Karlberg's attempt to vindicate Kline's construction of the Mosaic covenant. Although (relatively speaking) their analysis is an improvement on Karlberg, they still do not seem to have moved beyond his basic commitment to reading the tradition in light of or in reference to Kline" (39 n. 40).

25. There were numerous other objections that Kline had raised over the years against some of the faculty members of Westminster, including the Dillard-Longman-Enns school of hermeneutics, the multi-perspectivalism of John Frame and Vern Poythress, and Harvie Conn's contextualization of theology in various historical/societal/cultural settings.

In one of my internet postings (at Old Life Theological Society and Green Baggins) I had remarked: "Is there a suggestion here that *Westminster III* (after the dismissal of Enns and Green by the Lillback regime) is back on track, having returned to the glorious days of 'Machen and the fundamentalists,' i.e., those bearing the Westminster orthodoxy of

Study Republication" is a travesty.[26] One would hope that a newly-appointed committee of the OPC would redress the grievous wrong that has been committed with regard to this committee's reading of the work of Kline and

the founding faculty? The prominent issues here are twofold: (1) biblical inerrancy; and (2) the doctrine of salvation (specifically, justification by faith alone). Of course, *Westminster I* came to an inglorious end with the departure of Professor Meredith Kline. Happily, he did leave an indelible imprint upon Westminster in California. This now raises the pressing question whether or not Westminster West remains unambiguously at odds with the new theological direction taken at Westminster East. What direction, you ask? Does Westminster West denounce unequivocally elements of semi-Barthianism that has gained widespread ground within Reformed circles today and within evangelical Protestantism more broadly, notably as regards the teaching on 'eschatological' justification and election? The question is whether or not Westminster West will commit unreservedly and uncompromisingly to clear, consistent teaching upholding the *fundamentals of Reformed orthodoxy,* that borne by Old Westminster. The test case is now front and center in the dispute within the Orthodox Presbyterian Church regarding to the classic Reformed doctrine of 'republication' (what is the peculiar role of 'law' in the Mosaic Covenant)." For more on this, see my "Current Study on Republication: Where Matters Presently Stand" (http://www.trinityfoundation.org/update.php?id=2).

The closing paragraph of "The Committee for the Study of Republication: 2013 Address to the Presbytery of the Northwest" reads: "Because of the limit of authority with which the Confession [WCF] can speak on the subject, members of this Presbytery are called upon to use modesty and humility in dispute and to recognize the present volatile situation as an opportunity for displaying true Christ-like virtues. It should also be remembered that the world is watching, and that anything less than the above attitude will not only lead to further fissures and distraction within the church, but is bound to deliver ammunition to those who are outside, who have long judged the OPC to be sectarian and narrow-minded. Such charges are at times well deserved and at times fueled by sheer ignorance, but we must be intentional about avoiding needless offences. Undue controversy over issues such as republication may not be conductive to or may even hinder our mission to the world" (https://sites.google.com/site/mosaiccovenant/home).

Peter A. Lillback in *Seeing Christ in All of Scripture: Hermeneutics at Westminster Theological Seminary* (Peter A. Lillback, editor; Philadelphia: Westminster Seminary Press, 2016): http://westminsterseminarypress.com/) explains: "Thus, this little work is presented to the public as an introduction to the hermeneutical method that today characterizes the biblical scholarship of the Westminster faculty" (4). He further comments: "The Christ-centered manner in which the Reformed hermeneutical method engaged Scripture developed out of the unifying principle of the covenant" (5). (He disingenuously cites WCF, chapter 7 (two covenant, works and grace.) He then concludes: "These classic Reformed emphases on the covenantal unity of the Bible highlight the necessity of an organic Christ-centered interpretation of Scripture. All of Westminster Theological Seminary's faculty and board members have committed to this confessional hermeneutic since the seminary's founding" (6). Such has clearly not been the case.

26. It is apparent that much of the analysis in this report regurgitates the thinking found in the book *Merit and Moses.*

Section Three: Departure from Historic Reformed Federalism

restate the biblical teaching pertaining to the covenants, giving priory to Scripture rather than the *Confession*.

Addendum: Bibliographical Note

Much has been written elucidating both the history and the interpretation of Reformed covenant theology. I have devoted a career in this undertaking. The special focus of my four closely-knit books published by Wipf and Stock—compilations of articles and book reviews—details developments at Westminster Seminary (East and West) regarding the doctrines of justification by faith alone (*sola fide*), election, and the covenants. Since the early twentieth century, the Westminster seminaries have been the conveyers of the theological and confessional tradition, which was given formative expression at the Assembly that convened at Westminster in London, England (1643–49). Each volume builds upon the previous one, providing additional, timely evidence and documentation of changes which have taken place at (New) Westminster, notably, as that pertains to deviant teaching respecting the two formative principles of the Protestant Reformation, the formal (the doctrine and interpretation of Scripture) and the material (the doctrine of salvation by grace through faith).

Covenant Theology in Reformed Perspective: Collected Essays and Book Reviews in Historical, Biblical, and Systematic Theology (2000): Central to my research and publications over the course of four decades, beginning with my graduate studies in New Testament (ThM) and in historical/systematic theology (ThD/PhD), is the subject of Reformed interpretation of the Mosaic Covenant as an administration of the "Covenant of Grace," extending from the Fall to the Consummation (the second coming of Christ). Related topics include the following: the relation of the two God-ordained institutions, church and state, in the period of common grace (thus in distinction from the circumstance of the ancient Israelite theocracy in the period from Moses to the first coming of Christ); the distinction between the original "Covenant of Works" established with Adam as created in the image of God and the subsequent "Covenant of Grace" (including the intra-trinitarian "Covenant of Redemption"); biblical typology as taught in the Old and New Testaments; and the intimate bond between amillennial covenant theology and biblical eschatology (reflecting the "already/not yet" structure of redemptive history and its application to individual salvation by virtue of union with Christ).

Gospel-Grace: The Modern-Day Controversy (2003): The first sequel to *Covenant Theology in Reformed Perspective*—what is foundational to all subsequent publications—addresses the rapidly-growing opposition in evangelical-Reformed scholarship to traditional, historic Protestant teaching (*a la* Lutheran and Reformed orthodoxy) concerning the antithesis between two principles of inheritance, works and (gospel-)grace. The twofold doctrine of the covenants, the Covenant of Works and the Covenant of Grace, a staple in Reformed teaching, is upheld as essential to the system of Reformed orthodoxy, not an aberrant accretion of later "scholasticism." Criticism of radically new teachings emanating from Westminster Seminary, reflective of changes taking place in evangelical theology more broadly, is carefully assessed in these pages. Pivotal in this analysis and exposé is the teaching of Professors Norman Shepherd and Richard Gaffin. Coordinate with other developments in Westminster's department of systematic theology is the novel introduction of "multi-perspectivalism" crafted by John Frame and contextualization in the missional theorizing of Harvie Conn.

Federalism and the Westminster Tradition: Reformed Orthodoxy at the Crossroads (2006): The third in the series opens with a "commissioned" article, entitled "The Significance and Basis of the Covenant of Works: Exegetical and theological factors." It concludes with a discussion of the present-day challenge and confrontation within the church and the academy. The exemplary work of biblical theologians Geerhardus Vos and Meredith G. Kline, on the one hand, has provided needed amplification and clarification pertaining to aspects of Reformed exposition of the covenants of God in the twentieth and twenty-first centuries, marking a genuine advance in the history of doctrine. Thus, the picture is not altogether bleak; there are assuredly rays of hope and evidence of unwavering, deep-seated conviction regarding both the veracity and the integrity of the theology of the Westminster divines in some quarters today, all for the benefit of the church for generations to come. Yet, on the other hand, the result of years of deviant theological training at Westminster Seminary (Philadelphia) is evident in the mounting upheaval and polarization within the Orthodox Presbyterian Church, which has had from its inception the closest of ties to Westminster Seminary. The battle for the truth of Scripture begun in the age of the Protestant Reformation is therefore ongoing.

Engaging Westminster Calvinism: The Composition of Redemption's Song (2013): Unique in the theological literature, this conclusion to my four-volume study of Reformed covenant theology combines my work as

Section Three: Departure from Historic Reformed Federalism

a theological writer and teacher and my career in church music. Further analysis of the contentious struggle over the Reformed orthodox doctrine of the covenants and justification by faith alone (the inheritance-principle informing the Covenant of Grace, antithetical to the works-inheritance-principle undergirding the Covenant of Works) serves as prelude to the current crisis within the Orthodox Presbyterian Church, one having ramifications extending well beyond her borders across the evangelical-Reformed world. These studies of mine, among others, have helped precipitate the action of the 2014 General Assembly of the denomination in erecting a five-member study committee in an attempt to resolve the issues now dividing the churches (chiefly, its pastors and teachers). Grasping aright that which is the heart of the Gospel—justification by faith, apart from the works of the law—is requisite for the church's singing of the New Song for time and eternity. As it turns out, understanding the role and practice of music in the service of the church depends upon a proper interpretation of the revelation of God as the "theophanic Glory" and the church's place in the history of redemptive revelation. Here again, the essential and vital distinction between common grace and special grace informs our analysis.

Chapter Seven

The Protestant Reformation Derailed

Closing a Chapter in the Still-Ongoing Theological Dispute

RELEASE OF THE 2016 General Assembly study paper of the Orthodox Presbyterian Church[1] marks the ("official"[2]) conclusion of the four-decade-old controversy at Westminster Seminary and in the OPC. Mention, let alone discussion, of this paper among members of this ecclesiastical communion has been negligible. As a denominational "study report" written for the benefit of the entire constituency of the OPC, it is unlikely many have bothered to read this very lengthy, tediously written paper. Among notables outside the OPC, Cornelis Venema has followed very closely the

---

1. It is entitled, "Report of the Committee to Study Republication." As I have noted elsewhere, "Scott Clark addresses [in his recent posting] the problem of the misinterpretation of the relationship between Old and New Testaments (or the matter of the contrast between Moses and Christ as regards the diverse administrations of the single, ongoing Covenant of Grace in redemptive history). Curiously, Clark confronts the erroneous teachings of Dispensationalism, and not a word is said about the theological confusion today in the Reformed schools and churches closer to home. Foremost I have in mind the dispute in the Orthodox Presbyterian Church." See my posting, "It is a curious thing! More on the Republication Controversy" in *The Aquila Report,* May 4, 2017 (http://theaquilareport.com/curious-thing-republication-controversy/).

2. This is my reading of the issuance of this report (in light of developments within the OPC); although committee reports of General Assembly are not equivalent in authority or standing to the subordinate standards of the Reformed church (the Westminster Confession of Faith and Catechisms), in this case the study report is meant to close discussion concerning the longstanding, divisive controversy within her membership.

113

Section Three: Departure from Historic Reformed Federalism

long-standing controversy over the years.[3] As I argued in my own critique of the study report ("Troubler of Israel: Report on Republication by the Orthodox Presbyterian Church Assessing the Teaching of Professor Meredith G. Kline"[4]), I view the paper (to my great dismay) to be an utter travesty. Presently, it stands unchallenged in this ecclesiastical body.

General Assembly reports purport to be "thoughtful and weighty treatises on important matters but they are not constitutional documents. Only the Confession of Faith and Catechisms, the Form of Government, the Book of Discipline, and the Directory for the Public Worship of God of the Orthodox Presbyterian Church express the church's official understanding of what the Word of God teaches" (taken from OPC website). It turns out the 2016 paper is not for study and discussion. Instead, the message from the leadership has been: read, submit, and don't ask questions! Silence has become the strategy employed across the denomination, and picked up across the wider Reformed community sharing close ties to Westminster Seminary, East and West. It appears that the moratorium had been set in place months before the release of the OPC Report, one which continues, for the most part, to this day. Rather than denounce the teachings of Norman Shepherd and his closest ally, Richard Gaffin (co-author of the new theology), the committee which wrote this report has presented a thoroughly disported picture of the dispute, most notably as regards teaching concerning the republication of the original Covenant of Works *in modified form* under Moses, the covenant with theocratic Israel.

---

3. See my discussion of Venema below. Some have portrayed this raging dispute as purely "intramural," in an attempt to minimize the gravity of the theological issues debated. Nothing could be further from the truth: What is at stake are some of the essentials of the Christian faith, specifically, the nature of our union with Christ and the benefits that accrue from that union (e.g., justification by faith, eternal security, and assurance of salvation—all as manifestations of decretive election).

4. See chapter six. The OPC's Presbytery of the Northwest had been deeply divided in very contentious debates over the doctrine of republication. As recorded in the summary of proceedings of the 2017 General Assembly of the OPC regarding the conclusion of the Special Committee's visitation to the Presbytery of the Northwest over a period of two years: "Mr. Van Dyke reported for the Special Committee to visit the Presbytery of the Northwest, and recommended that the special committee be dissolved. The AC 9 reported silence on the report and its recommendations. The motion to dissolve the committee with thanks was approved by the assembly" (from the OPC website: http://www.opc.org/GA/84th_GA_rpt.html?pfriendly=Y&ret=LodBLzgodGhfRoFfcnBoLmh obWw%3D). Here again we encounter *silence:* No discussion or dissent regarding the OPC's position-paper on republication and its reading of the theology of Meredith Kline.

Some have turned a blind eye to the controverted Shepherd-Gaffin theology widespread in the OPC; others have embraced the new teaching. This has resulted in theological corruption now deeply imbedded within the OPC and within Westminster Seminary in Philadelphia, once the bastion of Reformed orthodoxy. (Since the beginnings of the denomination, it had held the closest of ties to the seminary.) Various "excuses" have been offered for Gaffin's unrelenting, vigorous support and endorsement of Shepherd's heterodox teaching. Chief among these: (1) Gaffin's close friendship with Shepherd (which obviously counts more than fidelity to Scripture—this from the one who would come to assume the systematics post at the seminary and who would come to yield the greatest influence in the seminary and in the OPC); and (2) Gaffin supposedly grew in his understanding of problems inherent in Shepherd's teaching. Others have engaged in the deliberate, calculated, misleading imposition of orthodox teaching into Gaffin's formulations. False on all accounts. The OPC prides herself on her orthodoxy; regrettably, many of her leaders and members end up offering lip-service to the Westminster Standards, all the while commending reformulations (however subtle for many) at crucial points in the Reformed theological system. For most, it is beyond the pale of reason to think that the OPC and the Westminster Seminary are guilty of deception and collusion on a grand scale. Likewise, faculty members of Westminster Seminary California have shown reticence, if not refusal, to denounce Gaffin's equally unorthodox theology, chiefly regarding his interpretation of justification by faith and works and his denial of the (classic) doctrine of the Covenant of Works.

As it turns out, the dispute over the doctrine of "republication," as it has been dubbed, is the most important, single issue in the debates at Westminster since the mid-1960s. The new interpretation regarding the doctrine of justification by faith and works and the doctrine of mutable election are the immediate fruits of a defective doctrine of the original Covenant of Works with Adam as federal head of all humankind. As I have recently summarized elsewhere:

> What exactly is at issue in these several mutations of "evangelical" theology? Central to the debate is the biblical (Reformed) doctrine of the Covenant of Works established by God with Adam as federal head of humanity and reestablished *in modified form* under Moses (i.e., adjusted to the post-Fall context, consistent with the progressive unfolding of the Covenant of Grace). There is only one way of salvation in the old and new economies of redemption—that is by

faith in Jesus Christ as Mediator of the covenant made with God's elect (and with them alone). Faith is the sole instrument appropriating the perfect righteousness of Christ, the Second Adam, imputed to the elect of God. The law of Moses—the covenant made at Sinai with theocratic Israel—imposes the works-inheritance principle operative in the original covenant with Adam. This time, however, the works-principle pertains *only* to the temporal occupation of the land of Canaan, originally given as an act of divine grace to theocratic Israel (the theocracy exemplifying a time of *national election,* rather than decretive election to salvation). The expulsion of Israel from Canaan in the time of her Babylonian captivity was due to covenant transgression; the return to the land was an act of God's grace, not based on Israel's merit (including repentance from sin, though requisite). Had the governing principle of the covenant with Moses been that of grace, Israel's sins would have been fully and entirely covered by the sacrifice of the Messiah who was to come. Israel would not have been exiled. Clearly a different principle of inheritance was at work, a principle antithetical to that of faith (redemptive grace). This teaching is summed up in the opposition of the Law and the Gospel, the unanimous tenet of historic, orthodox Protestantism.[5]

To be sure, theological controversy throughout the history of the Christian church provides the context for doctrinal formulation and restatement. The key to interpretation of the doctrine of the covenants in Scripture is the proper reading of the works-inheritance principle in the Mosaic covenant with theocratic Israel. Mainstream Reformed theology correctly teaches that the works-principle is antithetical to the grace-principle (operative in the Covenant of Grace, spanning the entire span of redemptive history).[6] In recent years many of those who view the operative, administrative principle in the Mosaic covenant (assuredly an administration of

---

5. See Mark W. Karlberg, *The Aquila Report,* May 4, 2017 (http://theaquilareport.com/curious-thing-republication-controversy/). On the other side of this dispute in contemporary Reformed theology, Sinclair B. Ferguson, in lectures given at Reformed Theological Seminary, offers this advice: "'Works' should not be viewed as the opposite of grace." Ferguson views the law-principle, "Do this and live," as a command having regard to sanctification, not justification (posted on the internet: http://johnowen.org/media/ferguson_owen_outline.pdf).

6. This argument was first introduced in Karlberg, "The Mosaic Covenant and the Concept of Works in Reformed Hermeneutics;" and "Reformed Interpretation of the Mosaic Covenant" (republished in my *Covenant Theology in Reformed Perspective*). Peter Golding, in *Covenant Theology,* generally follows my analysis, drawing heavily from my works without proper citation or quotation.

the single, overarching Covenant of Grace) as the principle of grace have slid into the Barthian camp by rejecting the biblical concept of "merit" (or "reward") associated with obedience to the covenant God originally made with humankind. They see the grace-principle functioning exclusively in the period before and after the sin of our first parents in the Garden. Consequently, these interpreters of Scripture have jettisoned the biblical and Reformed doctrine of the first Covenant of Works. Since there is no principle of merit in this modern-day exposition of the covenants, there is no reason not to view *faith and works* as "instrumental" in our justification before God. According to the new theology, human works or obedience does not merit the blessing of our heavenly Father, but is part of the "way of salvation" (such is the teaching of Shepherd and Gaffin). Likewise, the new take on God's covenant with Israel readily lends to the notion that election is *losable*, a major point emphasized by Shepherd.

Despite years of intense discussion and debate within Reformed orthodoxy, and the controversy surrounding the views of Shepherd (John Murray's hand-picked successor in the systematics department at Westminster Seminary), Cornelis Venema in his most recent publication, *Christ and Covenant Theology*,[7] continues to misread the history of federalism by substituting the Puritan doctrine of the Mosaic covenant (and its theonomic interpretation of church and state) for mainstream, historic Reformed covenant theology.[8] Venema's reading is simply wrong. And the crucial biblical text for the classic Protestant-Reformed antithesis between the Law and the Gospel, namely, Leviticus 18:5 (the OT text cited by the apostle Paul in order to elucidate the doctrine of justification by faith alone, i.e., apart from good works), is likewise distorted. According to Venema, the principle of law enunciated in Leviticus 18:5 is the principle of saving grace (here he confuses the necessary demonstration of obedience in the life of the believer associated with sanctification with the legal principle associated with a covenant-of-works arrangement). Though acknowledging the obedience

---

7. Published by P&R, which has been and remains essentially the publishing arm of Westminster Seminary in Philadelphia and of the OPC. Credit goes to Venema for pursuing discussion of this highly divisive subject in modern-day Reformed theology in genuine hope of reaching mutual understanding. Progress indeed has been made in achieving this aim. (More on this below.)

8. The writing of the Westminster Standards occurred on the eve of the ascendency of Puritanism in England. The Westminster divines did not attempt to resolve issues that were now emerging, notably, as regards divergent interpretations of the Mosaic Covenant. (Despite differences, there was underlying agreement on the Mosaic Covenant as an administration of the overarching Covenant of Grace.)

Section Three: Departure from Historic Reformed Federalism

of the Second Adam in the procurement of redemption for the elect of God as *meritorious*, Venema denies that the obedience of the First Adam would have earned the reward of life everlasting for himself and his progeny.[9] All of this results in the blatant misreading of the old, Mosaic economy and its relation to the new covenant inaugurated by Christ (entailing the abrogation of the legal principle regulative of life in the land of Canaan).

Does *Christ and Covenant Theology* offer any new or different analysis from what we read elsewhere in Venema's writings? Or it is essentially a regurgitation of his long-held views? Happily, this latest work does evidence some rethinking and reworking of prior formulations.[10] At the same time, however, Venema's analysis remains confusing, lacking in theological consistency. The book draws together previously published articles of the author—with some reworking of his critique and formulations.[11] This updated work, like previous writings of his, does not adequately engage the relevant theological literature on the subject at hand. And those who commend Venema's study (noted in the opening pages of the book) are all adherents of Murray's interpretation of the Mosaic Covenant. Dick Gaffin observes: "No one today is better qualified to address the perennially important issues of covenant theology than Cornel Venema. In this volume he considers some of these issues in the context of current discussions and debates, doing so in a particularly instructive and helpful manner." Mark Jones comments: "This is a book full of insightful commentary from Professor Venema. In places I rejoiced to see him correct some misunderstandings with his usual clarity and incisiveness." We do not find these assessments to be true, constructive, or helpful (given the long-standing controversy at Westminster and within the OPC). There is no reference to, let alone interaction with, the pivotal OPC report on republication; likewise, Venema's critique of Shepherd's theology (given the wide influence it has had) is lacking.[12] While Murray called for the

---

9. Ibid., 32–35.

10. Venema's analysis of the history of covenant theology and his own formulation of the doctrine of the covenants require further revision. Happily, his rethinking is moving in the right direction. He recognizes the gravity of the dispute we are confronting in Reformed theology today: "Perhaps the most pressing issue in contemporary discussion concerns the legitimacy of speaking of the prefall relationship between God and the human race in Adam as a covenant relationship, and one that may be properly denominated a 'covenant of works'" (ibid., 421).

11. The author informs his readers: "Most of the essays have been significantly revised—and, I hope, improved—for inclusion in this volume" (ibid., xxiv).

12. Venema prefers to zero in on the (heavy) "influence" of Kline upon many on the one side in the debate. If nothing else, Venema's analysis is wholly lopsided. In point

The Protestant Reformation Derailed

recasting of historic covenant theology, Venema misreads and misinterprets the tradition to suit his own formulations.[13] And in this book he still continues to misread Kline, the one who is Venema's leading opponent in this longstanding theological controversy.

In the "conclusion" (of all places!) Venema summarizes for his readers his current assessment of the controverted issues—after all is said and done. It is here that some crucial concessions are made by Venema. Here again is indication of further need on the part of the author for additional revision to this volume of collected writings. There does now appear to be something of a meeting of the minds regarding the fundamental concept of the "covenant of works." And for this we are most grateful. Most importantly, Venema concedes: "What distinguishes the prefall covenant of works from the postfall covenant of grace is the stipulated condition of perfect obedience to God's law on Adam's part, aside from which the life promised in the covenant would neither be retained nor advanced to a perfected fullness of eternal life" (423). He adds that "the central point of emphasis in the biblical depiction of this covenant is an obligation of obedience as the indispensable requirement for the realization of perfected communion with God in the state of glory."[14] *It is imperative that Venema avoid equivocation here: His remarks for and against the concept of "merit" as descriptive of the principle of law in the Covenant of Works amount to pure contradiction.* On the one

---

of fact, it was the Shepherd controversy, beginning in the mid-1970s, that stoked differences between Murray and Kline (what would later, after Shepherd's dismissal from Westminster Seminary, result in the irreconcilable differences between Gaffin on the one hand, and Karlberg and Kline, on the other). Actually, it was the late 1960s that mark the occasion of growing distaste for the Reformed doctrine of the Covenant of Works among some faculty members at the seminary. Kline once remarked to me that our battle would be "uphill all the way," and he has proven to be right. Assuredly, the thinking of Murray, Shepherd, and Gaffin has been the strongest influence at Westminster Seminary and within the OPC. Time and again, Shepherd and Gaffin have made their case with duplicity and concealment. Their plea for commitment to the teaching of Reformed orthodoxy has been disingenuous from the start. The strategy was to make Kline the target of attack, all in the effort to garner support their own deviant reading of the theological tradition. For Gaffin, the heterodoxy of Shepherd, Frame, and others never once factored in his argument against Kline's formulation.

13. Of course, Venema makes the counterchage: In his estimate, it is the proponents of the doctrine of republication who are judged guilty of misreading the Reformed tradition on the Mosaic Covenant. In point of fact, it is the Puritan stream of interpretation that was the new kid on the block. Discerning students will need to decide between these two readings of Reformed covenant theology (federalism), especially the distinctive teachings of English Calvinism.

14. *Christ and Covenant Theology*, 423.

SECTION THREE: DEPARTURE FROM HISTORIC REFORMED FEDERALISM

hand, Venema acknowledges: "Throughout the history of Reformed theology, a recurring issue in the doctrine of the covenants of works and of grace focuses upon the legitimacy of the language of 'merit' in the divine-human relationship that the covenant articulates."[15] He confusingly distinguishes between two kinds of merit, proper and improper. He insists that the obedience of Christ (the Second Adam) is properly meritorious, because he is the God-man. The obedience of the First Adam, had that been rendered in his time of probation, would only have been meritorious, "improperly speaking." And in conjunction with this, Venema continues to dichotomize an initial state of creation (nature) and a subsequent state of special relationship (covenant). In the state of nature God was under no obligation to extend Adam's life even if he remained an obedient son of God. The biblical doctrine of probation (with respect to the angelic host and the human race represented in Adam) teaches an altogether different picture of the justice of God in blessing and in curse. Nothing improper about the justice of God in blessing and in curse. (Venema's formulation is partly bogged by scholastic definition that runs counter to Scripture.)

Focusing on those aspects of Venema's discussion which address the doctrine of the Covenant of Works and the doctrine of "republication," we highlight three critical areas of ongoing debate among disputants. Firstly, Venema observes: "In the classic period of Reformed covenant theology, accordingly, the doctrine of the covenants of works and of grace provided a comprehensive biblical-theological account of the way human beings, created in God's image, obtain life and blessing in communion with the living God" (38–39). What is in view here, we must emphasize, is *eschatological* life and fellowship with God. At creation, Adam and Eve enjoyed communion with God. Successful probation would afford the blessing of life eternal (including confirmation in righteousness) based upon Adam's representative (federal) obedience. Venema observes: "Though it may be helpful to reserve the term 'grace' for God's unmerited favor toward undeserving sinners, there can be no objection to the claim that the Confession's language of 'voluntary condescension' refers to the *undeserved favor* God as Creator shows to his singles creature and image-bearers" (28). *This marks a change in Venema's formulation. But here we must exercise care in our exposition. Further definition/clarification is still necessary.* Venema's contention that

---

15. Ibid. Rather than perpetuate speculative notions repeatedly aired in scholastic Reformed federalism (notions derived from medieval scholasticism), the time has come to remedy the error and confusion inherent in our theological tradition. We are arguing for a genuine improvement in the theological formulation of the covenants.

Adam's original enjoyment of God was "undeserved" is wholly inaccurate and inappropriate. Creation surely is a work of God's goodness and beneficence; but there is no issue here of Adam somehow being "undeserving" of this creative (covenantal) act of God's kindness to humankind. Adam was created in perfect righteousness and holiness. By way of obedience, Adam would secure for himself and all his posterity the promised blessing of everlasting life as a matter of meritorious reward (earning). This is the essence of the traditional Protestant law/grace antithesis. The issue here is not semantic, but a matter of biblical definition (definition that is faithful to Scripture, not speculative or rationalistic).[16]

Secondly, although Venema differs with Murray on restricting the idea of "covenant" to that of *redemptive provision*, he agrees with him on the Mosaic economy as devoid of the works-inheritance principle. Venema contends: "The language of a 'works principle' is characteristically Klinean, but is not found among writers of the orthodox period in Reformed theology so far as I have been able to determine."[17] This ultimately leads Venema is dissolve the law/grace contrast drawn by the apostle Paul in Galatians 3:12, a citation of Leviticus 18:5. *Such is an example of Venema's eisegesis; it is not good biblical exegesis.* The hermeneutic employed here helps explain why Venema gives a passing grade to S.G. DeGraaf and G.C. Berkouwer, rather than placing their views decisively in the Barthian camp (with regard

---

16. The problem introduced by Venema is an echo of the medieval, scholastic nature/grace dichotomy. In point of fact, the (biblical) notion of *meritum ex pacto* is identical to the biblical concept of "strict justice," which Venema mistakenly rejects. See his additional comment (*Christ and Covenant Theology*, 28 n.37).

17. Ibid., 72 n.19. For discussion of the "works" concept in Reformed theology, see my dissertation, "The Mosaic Covenant and the Concept of Works in Reformed Hermeneutics." Regrettably, Venema quotes from O. Palmer Robertson: "Kline's definition of the Mosaic covenant as a covenant of meritorious works is also flawed by its effort to make a radical distinction between the basic nature of the Abrahamic and David covenant in comparison with the Mosaic covenant" (ibid., 129). Robertson sustains a blind eye with respect to Kline's restatement of the biblical covenants. It is true that Kline did reformulate views previously expressed in *By Oath Consigned*. The reason I refer so frequently to the superlative works of Kline is his mastery of (Vossian) biblical theology and his uncompromising commitment to the teaching of historic Reformed federalism. *Together we are building on a grand theological tradition, one that has been assailed since the time of Karl Barth.* Professor Kline is a man of great theological statue in our generation, having unique insight into the teaching of Scripture. He has not been given the recognition he deserves. Together he and I have labored to bring needed clarity and refinement ("exactness") to formulations in our theological tradition. To reiterate, there is pressing need to address the ambiguity, even contradiction, in Reformed interpretation since the days of the Protestant Reformation regarding the doctrine in dispute.

Section Three: Departure from Historic Reformed Federalism

to their rejection of the classic Protestant law/grace contrast). Accordingly, Venema warns: "It is especially important that critics of the WCF, especially those who write from within the framework of a commitment to historic Reformed orthodoxy, not unwittingly join their voices to those who do not share this commitment and whose criticism arise out of a radically unbiblical framework."[18] According to the express testimony of Scripture (specifically, the OT historical record and witness to the gospel of justification by faith), the old and new covenants are chiefly, but not exclusively, characterized by two contrasting principles of inheritance—works and faith (law and grace). Venema is correct in noting: "For Reformed theologians influenced by Kline, it is seen necessary to insist upon the republication in some sense of the covenant of works during the Mosaic economy in order to provide a solid basis for the articulation of Christ's saving and meritorious obedience in the covenant of grace."[19] While there is reference to the OPC study report on justification,[20] there is no mention of the denominational report on republication. Lacking also is thoroughgoing criticism of Shepherd's doctrine of the covenants. This amounts to an attempt at rewriting the history of the controversy at Westminster and in the OPC.

Thirdly, the study of typology rightly formulated confirms the Reformed doctrine of amillenialism. Venema's conception of this crucial discipline in biblical studies is far too restrictive and too limiting. Venema fails to do justice to the organic nature of the progressive unfolding of the Covenant of Grace over the course of redemptive history, notably, the transition from old to new economies of redemption. The movement from seed to full flowering fully justifies Kline's employment of the contrast between typical and antitypical spheres of life within the Mosaic economy. Israel's obedience, at times, did serve as typological examples of the messianic Servant of the Lord who was to come (blessing for obedience). Here it warrants noting Venema's failure to read and interact with other writings of Kline, such as *Glory in Our Midst* and *Har Magedon*.[21] These later works are vital in understanding the role of symbolism and typology in biblical exegesis and of the eschatological movement from old to new economies in the history of

---

18. Ibid., 36. It is all too clear that Venema also gives a pass to Shepherd, despite their strong differences on the doctrine of the covenants. In a word, Shepherd's doctrine of covenant and justification is heretical, judged in the light of Scripture and tradition.

19. Ibid., 424.

20. Van Drunen, et al., *Justification*.

21. The first is an exposition of the night visions of Zachariah, the second Kline's final, mature exposition of the doctrine of the covenants.

redemptive revelation in the thinking of Kline. Much more can be said, but we refer the reader here to writings of mine and others discussing covenant theology from the standpoint of biblical and systematic theology, and from the standpoint of the history of Reformed doctrine. (In my own published works I have attempted to view the doctrine of the covenants from all angles, and from the standpoint of all the relevant theological disciplines.)

Summing up, Venema's chief argument is the following. There is no merit (works) principle operating in the Mosaic economy of redemption (as part of the ongoing Covenant of Grace); and there is no merit (works) principle in the original Adamic covenant. Venema only recognizes *non-meritorious human work* (i.e., unrewarded obedience, or obedience as the expression of gratitude to God for his gifts in creation and redemption). Such is the way of the covenant.[22] Acknowledgment of the historical demarcation between the Fall and the subsequent period is insufficient in safeguarding the law/grace contrast. Venema's view of Christ's *unique* merit in fulfilling the original Covenant of Works undermines the parallel the apostle Paul draws between the First and Second Adams. (Here Venema's view is similar to that of Murray's.[23]) This conceptualization militates against the classic Protestant antithesis between the Law and the Gospel, despite Venema's claims to hold to such a contrast. And although Venema's inconsistent formulation falls within the pale of orthodoxy (as does Murray's), his position is theologically unstable. His repudiation of the doctrine of "republication" in connection with the Mosaic covenant opens up the way to insuperable theological problems for the interpretation of the old covenant, the covenant which has passed away with the inauguration of the new and better covenant in Christ. Were God's covenant with theocratic Israel an administration of pure grace (with no work-inheritance principle), Israel's transgression (one and all) would have been forgiven in Christ: There would have been no exile, no judgment placed upon Israel of old. By sovereign design, all of Israel (including those individuals who were recipients of the indefectible life in Christ, i.e., eternal salvation) suffered the curse of exile from the promised land of Canaan. According to the Book of Deuteronomy, the blessings and curses were promulgated to the nation of Israel as a theocratic entity. The law of Moses served as ancient Israel's pedagogue and schoolmaster to bring her to God; this principle of law-inheritance was abrogated with the coming of Christ. How Venema

---

22. This is all too reminiscent of Shepherd's formulations.
23. *Christ and Covenant Theology*, 22.

SECTION THREE: DEPARTURE FROM HISTORIC REFORMED FEDERALISM

and others in the Murray camp can ignore the plain teaching of Scripture is the Great Enigma!

Returning one final time to theological developments at Westminster Seminary, the initial uproar over Shepherd's classroom teaching in the mid-1970s arose over his doctrine of soteric justification. It was not until 1977 onwards that Kline and Karlberg had recaptured the teaching of mainstream Reformed tradition regarding the Covenant of Works made with Adam and reissued in modified form with theocratic Israel. It was at this time that focus shifted more directly to the older Reformed doctrine of the republication of the works-inheritance principle in the Mosaic covenant. Prior to this time the views of John Murray on the Mosaic covenant (including Murray's denial of the classic doctrine of the Covenant of Works) had gained prominence among faculty and students of Westminster.[24]

---

24. Ligon Duncan upholds the doctrine of the Covenant of Works as well as Murray's interpretation concerning the Mosaic covenant. At the same time, Duncan acknowledges the Barthian influence on Murray's theology of the covenants (see: http://www.fpcjackson.org/resource-library/classes-and-training/covenant-of-works-and-covenant-of-grace; and http://www.fpcjackson.org/resource-library/classes-and-training/the-mosaic-covenant). Andrew Woolsey's 1988 dissertation *Unity and Continuity in Covenantal Thought* (Glasgow University) was published in 2012 by Reformation Heritage Books with the same title, *Unity and Continuity in Covenantal Thought: A Study in the Reformed Tradition to the Westminster Assembly*. The published study is somewhat dated, in that it does not interact with literature since 1988 (hence, no analysis of the Shepherd-Gaffin school of interpretation or anything subsequent). Compare also, Robert Letham, "'Not a Covenant of Works in Disguise' (Herman Bavinck)." Both Woolsey and Letham acknowledge the importance of the doctrine of the Covenant of Works, and both authors follow Murray's interpretation of the Mosaic covenant, denying the administrative works-merit principle.

Woolsey's study is an analytic, encyclopedic review of exponents of the Reformed doctrine of the covenants. Lacking any original thinking on the part of the author, it is at times a superficial reading of the sources (both primary and secondary). Essentially, the book is a regurgitation of the plethora of views held by Reformed expositors (all sharing the essentials of Reformed teaching on the covenants). Once again, we find Woolsey's reading at times to be contradictory, indicating failure on his part to evaluate rightly parts of Reformed teaching in need of clarification and correction (as I have long argued). Woolsey's findings does confirm my analysis and my plea for (minor) revision of the Reformed doctrine of the covenants, specifically as concerns the Mosaic Covenant and the operative concept of works/merit in the typological sphere of life in Canaan. Some of the major convictions of Woolsey regarding the doctrine of the covenants include these: (1) espousal of the nature/covenant dichotomy in the state of creation (2) denial of the doctrine of "meritorious" reward (which leads him to posit erroneously two kinds of grace, pre-fall and post-fall); and (3) acknowledgement within the tradition of the prominence of the doctrine of republication of the covenant of works under Moses (utilizing the classic Reformed-Protestant law/gospel antithesis wherein the concept of

Kline and Karlberg made diligent application of insights drawn from three inter-related disciples in the theological curriculum—biblical theology, systematics, and the history of doctrine. Early on, I held great appreciation for the teaching of Shepherd and Gaffin, only to part ways over the years as the issues in the raging dispute on the seminary campus (and beyond) became more disruptive. Half way through my doctoral studies Shepherd requested of me that he discontinue his appointment as my doctoral advisor; and being granted, Robert Godfrey then assumed the supervisory position. Several years after the obtainment of my doctorate at Westminster, church historian Clair Davis referred to me a later doctoral student of his, Jeong Koo Jeon. Jeon and I shared many long hours of discussion relating to Reformed covenant theology. That led to several publications by Jeon (many with Wipf and Stock Publishers).

Over the years Westminster Seminary in Philadelphia has lost its theological footing. The biblical department was led down very different paths through the work of Raymond Dillard (carried on by Tremper Longman and Peter Enns in OT, and Moisès Silva and Dan McCartney in NT); the theology department followed the Shepherd path under Gaffin (colleagues included, among others, Sinclair Ferguson, Tim Trumper, David Garner, and Lane Tipton); and the church history department followed suit under Peter Lillback and Carl Trueman. *Reforming the Christian Faith*, the fifth work of mine published by Wipf and Stock, brings closure to my case study of Westminster Seminary (specifically, my critique of the still,

---

law is "strictly" interpreted in its antithesis to redemptive grace—analogous to Calvin's teaching on the Law/Spirit contrast with reference to the old and new covenants).

At the same time, Woolsey provides scant attention to the Mosaic economy of redemption more broadly, beyond discussion of the unity of the Covenant of Grace in redemptive history. He holds essentially to the views of John Murray on redemptive covenants. In the final analysis, Woolsey's study is short on theological analysis, failing to engage the issues in dispute to any great extent, except to defend the integrity and unity of historic Reformed scholasticism (for which we are truly grateful). The "Foreword" by Richard A. Muller hails this study as "the first major attempt in English to present a view of the movement of Reformed thought on the covenant from its Reformation origins to the more detailed formulations of the early to mid-seventeenth century." Muller remains on the wrong side of the contemporary dispute regarding the "covenant of works" (and the "merit" concept), and as regards the Mosaic administration of the ongoing Covenant of Grace, which both Woolsey and Muller assiduously avoid discussing to any great extent. Failure to grasp the characteristic function of law (as works-principle) operative in the Mosaic economy of redemption leads to confusion, even contradiction, regarding the place of faith and obedience in redemptive covenant (justification and sanctification). Such is the liability of espousing the misinterpretation view of the Mosaic covenant.

Section Three: Departure from Historic Reformed Federalism

ongoing controversy at the seminary, in the OPC, and in the Reformed ecclesiastical community-at-large. Sadly, the dispute remains unresolved.[25] As I noted my earlier internet posting:

> Of historical note: The congregation of First Presbyterian Church, North Shore (Ipswich, MA) has transferred to the Presbyterian Church in America.[26] This may well be the beginning of another exodus out of the OPC, a rupture well justified. The division within the Westminster community (including that between the Westminster Seminaries, East and West) originates out of the heterodox teachings of Norman Shepherd and Richard Gaffin, *not* from the differences between John Murray and Meredith Kline on the covenants (the latter differences pale to insignificance in comparison with the new, unorthodox teaching that continues to gain advocacy in the Reformed camp today). The Shepherd-Gaffin theology has jettisoned the Reformed doctrine of the Covenant of Works (wherein the works-merit principle is operative) and the doctrine of justification by faith (apart from the good works of the believer). On the eve of the 500th anniversary of the Protestant Reformation, such erroneous teaching as this must be eradicated from our schools and churches. The OPC study on republication has done a great disservice to the denomination and to the Reformed community at large. Needed are a few brave, and faithful men ("courageous Calvinists" as they have of late been dubbed) to lead at this critical time in the history of the Reformed churches in America and world-wide.[27]

---

25. See the featured essay in *New Horizons* by Dick Gaffin, "For Us and for Our Salvation," 3–5. The phrase quoted in the title of the article is taken from the Nicene Creed. The essay serves as the latest summary the Shepherd-Gaffin understanding of justification and sanctification (or, more generally, the doctrine of union with resurrected Christ). In this essay there is no mention of the sole instrumentality of faith in justification (given the fact the doctrine of justification by faith has been at the center of ongoing controversy). Rather we read more of the same points Gaffin has been making for years—all serving to complement, rather than challenge, the views of Shepherd. It was Clair Davis who noted in his classroom lectures the repeated pattern in church history that once orthodox seminaries typically last fifty years before heterodoxy sets in. This has surely proved to be the case at Westminster.

26. This is the congregation with whom Dr. Kline and his family worshipped.

27. Karlberg, *The Aquila Report* (see footnote 5 above). Historian Darryl Hart continues to view the OPC through the lens of stalwart J. Gresham Machen, founder of the denomination; Hart resists any notion that there are now grave theological deviations within this ecclesiastical communion affecting the fundamentals of the biblical, Reformed faith. Most recently, see https://oldlife.org/2017/06/14/where-do-you-go-when-you-leave-progressive-presbyterianism/.

Rather than ministering as faithful, conscientious under-shepherds of Christ's flock, far too many have proved to be wolves in sheep's clothing, deceiving the uninformed and the misinformed. The time has come, however, to move on: The next generation or two will need to found new churches and schools (or, at the very least, form new educational and ecclesiastical alliances). After forty years or more, the OPC has shown herself to be incapable of cleaning house, guarding the biblical faith pertaining to essential Christian doctrine. Clearly the OPC continues to conceal, even promote, deviant theology at the very time we observe the 500th anniversary of the Protestant Reformation. The battle for truth is intense, and has been since the beginnings of church history. May God grant mercy and faithfulness in upholding the Gospel of saving grace and in the spread of historic, Reformed orthodoxy for future generations to come.

Epilogue

Christ, Church, and Covenant
Christian Calling in the Reformed Tradition

IN THIS CLOSING EPILOGUE we look at the relation between Christ, the Church (the Bride of Christ), and the Covenant of Grace—more exactly, the ordering of the life of the saints in the new covenant. Affirming the doctrines of the Reformed faith comes more easily than does application of biblical doctrine in the life of the congregation. Alongside this calling and responsibility (chiefly shared by teaching and ruling elders) is recognition that the spiritual governance of the local congregation by means of God's covenant is, to one degree or another, largely being neglected today or short-changed. The reason, not peculiar to our day, is the difficulty of implementation, its apparent "impracticality" (by a secular culture that ever threatens to shape the life and witness of the church). To be sure, the Reformed way of life is not palatable in a culture that is opposed to the exclusivity of the true faith. Truth be told, the ministry of the Gospel has never been easy. The revealed will of God confronts sinner and saint with the uncompromising call to follow Christ, to take up his cross daily. We are called to a life of holiness and righteousness in the midst of an evil and perverse society. And we are called to bear witness to the Christ of the Scriptures, the only savoir of sinners.

The proper purpose of redemptive covenant, from the period of the Fall to the Consummation, is the election to salvation of all those for whom Christ died. In the present (semi-eschatological) age, we are not to attempt to separate the elect from the non-elect, those who are members of the church "outwardly." We are not to separate the wheat from the tares within the household of faith. Such sifting awaits the end of the age. Membership in the visible church is an approximate realization of what is recorded in the Book of Life (comprising the number of those who are members of the church invisible). Christ, as the head of the church, has ordered the life of the godly in accordance with his Word. And the growth of the church is attained in a twofold manner: (1) the implementation of the "household principle" (not the principle of election); and (2) the evangelistic, missional outreach of the church in all the world. *The sacraments, baptism and the Lord's Supper, are the chief means for the administration and expansion of the church.* Fulfillment of the Great Commission involves the baptism of confessors, training in righteousness and obedience, and witness to all the world (Matt 28:18–20).

Central in corporate worship is the preaching of the Word, with application made to the needs of the local body, the flock of Christ (application of the Word always varies according to the immediate circumstances). Coordinate with biblical preaching is the establishment and maintenance of a well-developed program of Christian education for all ages. This too follows from the commandment given in Christ's Great Commission. Maturity in the faith, both individual and corporate, requires solid milk on which to feed. Compassionate, loving discipleship is also requisite for spiritual growth and maturity in the congregation. As the company of saints called out from the world to bear witness to the sovereign Lord of heaven and earth, they serve as ambassadors of Christ, ministering the fullness of grace by means of education, evangelism, and missions. The church as an institution is distinct from the state. The latter does not represent nor speak for the church, but is established by God for the exclusive purpose of maintaining the safety, health, and welfare of all its citizens. Only the church is a spiritual, confessional body.

The calling of church leaders is to train believers to think biblically, bringing all thought and action in subjection to God's Word as applied by the Spirit of Christ. To achieve this, recognition of and implementation of the two principles of Lutheran and Reformed Protestantism are of paramount importance. All doctrine and life are shaped by study of the Scriptures, the Old and New Testaments. A sound doctrine of Scripture as the Word of God (distinct from ecclesiastical tradition) and a sincere profession of the doctrine of justification by faith alone are all-determinative. Both require ongoing proclamation and defense, necessitating vigilance at every level of church government and life—in both the church and in the

Epilogue: Christ, Church, and Covenant

academy. As has been frequently noted: As the seminary goes, so goes the church. Ongoing study of the Scriptures is a mark of the true church. By these means summarized above, the church grows in spiritual maturity—in likeness to Jesus Christ, the "New Man." This includes equipping the saints for works of ministry within the body, varied and diverse as that is.

Finally, corporate worship is carried out in accordance with the so-called "regulative principle" as taught in Reformed theology. This vital principle of Christian worship brings into view the most important hour of the week, the gathering of the saints for corporate worship and witness. The essential ingredients in worship include the following: the reading of Scripture, prayer, the singing of hymns and songs, offerings to the Lord, the preaching and expounding the Word of God, and the proper administration of the sacraments of baptism and the Lord's Supper. To be sure, some measure of cultural diversity (notably with regard to musical styles) is to be recognized and to be encouraged. Several aspects of worship fall under the category of "circumstance." The use of instruments reflects the "cultural" expression of the worshipping congregation (here again diversity is evident). While the liturgy of Reformed worship is relatively uniform, there is room for some variation and difference. An important element in worship is congregational singing, the sung response of the saints to the mercy and compassion of our heavenly Father, who summons us to worship and fear him. Of course, central to corporate worship is the expounding of the Word of God. No element of worship must eclipse this (both in terms of the allocation of time and placement in the order of service). The power and beauty of music, notably its ability to give emotional expression to the passions of the human heart (such as joy, sorrow, thanksgiving, petition, and above all, praise) are conducive to praise and thanksgiving to God, an important aspect of spiritual discipline. Singing provides a medium for rendering heart-felt worship to God, giving utterance to the praises, supplications, and desires of worshippers in corporate witness to God's lordship, and as a means of sounding forth teachings contained in the inspired Word (see Colossians 3:16). Compositional style over the many centuries of church history is exceedingly rich and diversified. Congregational song is best served by the use of musical styles and idioms appropriate for and accessible to the worshipping saints. Church music serves as an important medium for making known the riches of God's mercy and grace. In the final analysis, musical style and composition in the local congregation is, in part, an expression of cultural tastes and artistic maturity.

Epilogue: Christ, Church, and Covenant

Since the time of the Protestant Reformation (and the advent of the use of the pipe organ in churches), there have been those who have opposed the use of choir and instruments as accompaniment for congregational song. They argue that though it did serve to distinguish worship in the Solomonic temple—in keeping with the symbolism and typology associated with the ancient theocracy and institution under Moses—it now has been entirely abrogated under the present age of the new covenant in Christ. Certain groups within the Reformed tradition (notably, the Genevan churches under Calvin, Scottish Presbyterians, and the Puritans in the Old and New England) had advocated exclusive, unaccompanied Psalm-singing. Other groups (like the Dutch Calvinists who produced an exceedingly rich repertoire of hymns and choral/organ compositions, many which reflect upon the Psalms) eagerly set about to convey the Christian message in musical language in the context of corporate worship. Theological arguments, Reformation and modern, have been made for both positions. We need not summarize them here, except to indicate that my position is one that encourages the use of choir and instruments, though these are not in any respect *essential* in corporate worship.[1]

Parenthetically, varied artistic styles are likewise reflected in church architecture—whatever the size and shape of the building in which worshippers meet. Architectural details and accoutrements are inevitable and welcome enhancements of the worship space. Obviously, religious and cultural tradition of one kind or another has a direct bearing upon architectural design. As one example, we might compare the exquisite architecture of the Presbyterian and Episcopal churches in Chestnut Hill, Pennsylvania, near where I live. Both stone structures—one with a tower, the other with a thin spire—register their special presence in the community, pointing earthly inhabitants heavenward. They stand as a daily reminder and witness to the spiritual relationship we have with the Creator of heaven and earth. The interior worship space of each captures in very different ways the beauty and holiness of standing in the presence of God, in the place where God meets with his people in corporate worship.[2] The structure of

---

1. The position of exclusive Psalm-singing, in my judgment, runs counter to the teaching of the New Testament. With the accomplished work of Christ in redemption—having begun with his earthly incarnation and ended with his ascension into heaven—we now sing the New Song, the Song of Christ. The Book of Psalms was the hymnal for ancient Israel. That witness and revelation have been modified by virtue of the advent of Christ and the addition of the corpus of writings known as the New Testament.

2. In his conversation with the Samaritan woman (John 4), Jesus explains the contrast

Epilogue: Christ, Church, and Covenant

the Presbyterian church in Chestnut Hill is striking is its simplicity, the Episcopalian in its magnificent, stunning craftsmanship of stained-glass windows and intricate wood designs. The question can be asked: Are both interiors appropriate and justified expressions of Christian faith, examples of wise stewardship? The answer will partly depend upon one's own tradition within Protestantism. Presbyterians (among whom I number) advocate for the former, simpler design.[3]

Returning to the subject of congregational song and church music more generally, we draw an important comparison between the Presbyterian and Anglican traditions in their historic and characteristic expressions. Musical compositions set to Scripture include hymns, anthems, and cantatas (among other forms). Liturgical music, in some church traditions, is designed to enhance and accentuate the "poetry" of Scripture and creed, broadly speaking, as well as draw attention to the awe and splendor of worshipping in the presence of the living God. The traditional Anglican liturgy is replete with biblical texts. The development of musical forms and styles in these churches is markedly diverse in scope, skill, and artistry.[4] The

---

between worship under the old and new economies of redemption in terms of the unique ministration of the Spirit. He speaks of new covenant worship as that which is realized "in Spirit and in truth." Thematically and theologically developed throughout John's Gospel and Apocalypse, the dawning of the new age (the age of the new covenant) is a decidedly eschatological (forward-looking) occurrence. The apostle John repeatedly draws the contrast between Old Testament types and New Testament realities. Typological worship in the Solomonic temple was uniquely symbolical of God's heavenly session with the saints (as well as his distance); in the new economy of redemption God is present wherever the saints gather in corporate worship. There is a heightened immediacy of God's dwelling this his redeemed people.

3. For a more general introduction, the reader is directed to the insightful article by Meredith G. Kline, "Symbols, Structures, and Scripture."

4. At a Christmas choral concert I had attended, a gentleman seated behind me recounted during intermission his pleasure of hearing the choir of Cantebury Cathedral (England), where the men sang on one side and the trebles on the other. He quipped: "I never better experienced a foretaste of heaven." How is that so? For the sons and daughters of God, the highest expression of praise is singing to the Lord. Though often neglected in preaching and teaching, one of the many attributes of God is beauty, and we his saints are called to worship God in the beauty of holiness. The title of one of the writings of the Christian art historian Hans Rookmaaker is *Art Needs No Justification*. The main thought in this treatise is this: The human spirit (notably, the creature refashioned in Christ as God's true image-bearer) is inevitably caught up in the splendor, awe and beauty of music (and art, more generally) that conveys truth and integrity. The work of the artist is to imitate the creativity of God and to reflect his grandeur. Whether we contemplate God's works in creation or in redemption, we are to give heartfelt expression to the glory and majesty God—with thanksgiving and by means of enthusiastic singing—voices joined

Epilogue: Christ, Church, and Covenant

following is excerpted from my prior article entitled "Theological Reflections on Church Music, Arts, and Architecture."[5]

> Presbyterian worship does not incorporate a "high" liturgy; that is to say, as a rule Presbyterians do not utilize set forms (notably fixed prayers, psalms and chants sung mostly by highly trained and highly skilled musicians). Nor in each and every service of Sunday morning worship do Presbyterians observe the Lord's Supper (called the "Mass" in high churches). Rather, Presbyterians give focus to the Word preached and to music sung by the congregation (with assistance by choral leadership that has prepared the music in advance of the service). Additionally, most Presbyterian congregations prefer amateur vocalists in choir and praise teams drawn from the membership of the church, rather than paid professionals—this for the sake of fully involving the congregation in worship and witness to the Word. Music in the church, rightly understood, places the privilege and the responsibility for singing God's praises and for lifting up songs of lament and supplication upon the worshippers. Music that is pleasing to God is never "performance," although vocalists and instrumentalists who help lead the congregation in song need to prepare well, offering the best of their God-given musical talents for the glory of God. (Unless there is talent to be utilized in worship leadership, there would be no need for choirs or praise teams. Musical talent properly exercised in the church provides encouragement and support for strong, vibrant congregational singing.)
>
> "Church cathedral music" is uniquely created for the acoustical space of the cathedral or large church. The Anglican view of choir and liturgical worship is drawn from the Old Testament—from the Levitical practice of ancient Israel in the time of the old Mosaic economy. Presbyterian doctrine, on the other hand, teaches that the Levitical practice is neither requisite nor commended for the worshipping saints under the new covenant established by Jesus Christ. Theologically speaking, form gives way to substance—or more accurately, shadow gives way to reality. The temple of Solomon (and its worship experience), grand and glorious as it was, and appropriate as it was for its time and place, has been superseded by the living temple of God, which is the Spirit of Christ himself dwelling in the very midst of the new covenant

together in worship to the One seated in the heavenlies. For helpful insights see the writing of Victoria Sirota, *Preaching to the Choir;* see also the several essays on church music in my *Engaging Westminster Calvinism.*

5. In Karlberg, *Engaging Westminster Calvinism,* 153–54.

Epilogue: Christ, Church, and Covenant

community. (The Shekinah glory in Old Testament times symbolized the greater glory of God to be revealed in the latter day, the day inaugurated at Pentecost.) Worship in the Solomonic temple was designed to create a distance between God and the worshipper entering the sanctuary in awe and fear. New covenant worship accentuates the intimacy of a father and his adopted family. Presbyterians take delight in the praises of God uttered from lips of Spirit-filled sons and daughters, those freely and graciously adopted into the family of God. By his grace new covenant worshippers have been freed from the terrors of the law. In the words of the hymn "Let Us Love and Sing and Wonder":

> *Let us love, and sing and wonder,*
> *let us praise the Savior's name!*
> *He has hushed the law's loud thunder,*
> *he has quenched Mount Sinai's flame:*
> *He has washed us with his blood,*
> *he has brought us nigh to God.*

Whatever our ecclesiastical tradition and whatever the style of music, it is incumbent upon church musicians to craft the best for corporate worship and witness to the Lord of all beauty, glory, and praise. Froth and triteness have no place in worship that is worthy of God, the Creator and Redeemer who is making all things new in Christ.

Christ, as head of his church, calls believers to worship "in Spirit and in truth" (John 4:24). Moving from the old Mosaic order of redemption to the new administration of the Covenant of Grace in the period between the two advents of Christ, we recognize the wholly spiritual character of the Body of Christ. Type and symbol give way to realized eschatology: The physical temple and all its accouterments no longer are the norm. Some flexibility remains in the use of art, choir, and vestments in new covenant worship. Such belong to the (cultural) circumstance of the gathered saints. The biblical canon regulative of the life and government of the church is the New Testament (the Old Testament remains a vital and essential part of the church's scriptures, the full, complete biblical witness of God's saving work in the world). And the chief means instituted by Christ for the establishment, government, and maintenance of the church are the sacraments of baptism and the Lord's Supper (compare again Matt 28:18–20). What distinguishes Reformed congregations from other Protestant communions is best reflected in her confessional symbols, notably, the Westminster

Epilogue: Christ, Church, and Covenant

Confession of Faith and the Larger and Shorter Catechism. In the Reformed tradition it is the doctrine of the covenants, both in terms of the history of redemptive revelation in Scripture and its formative role in church life and governance, which captures her unique witness to Christ and to his people, the redeemed of God.

Bibliography

Barth, Karl. *Church Dogmatics.* G. W. Bromiley and T. R. Torrance, eds. New York: Scribner, 1955–1962.

Beach, J. Mark. *Christ and the Covenants: Francis Turretin's Federal Theology as a Defense of the Doctrine of Grace.* Göttingen: Vandenhoeck & Ruprecht, 2007.

Beale, Gregory. *A New Testament Biblical Theology: The Unfolding of the Old Testament in the New.* Grand Rapids: Baker, 2011.

Berkhof, Hendrikus. *Christian Faith: An Introduction to the Study of the Faith.* Grand Rapids: Eerdmans, 1979.

Berkhof, Louis. *Systematic Theology.* Fourth revised edition. Grand Rapids: Eerdmans, 1941.

Brown, Mark. *Christ and the Condition: The Covenant Theology of Samuel Petto (1624–1711).* Grand Rapids: Reformation Heritage, 2012.

Brown, Michael, and Zach Keele. *Sacred Bond: Covenant Theology Explored.* Grandville, MI: Reformed Fellowship, 2012.

Collingridge, Mark A., and Brett A. McNeill. *Republication: A Biblical, Confessional and Historical Defense.* Paper submitted to the Presbytery of the Northwest, OPC. Available on PDF: http://pnwopc.org/wp-content/uploads/2013/10/Republication-Paper-Final-Draft.pdf.

Cocceius, Johannes. *The Doctrine of the Covenant and Testament of God.* Translated by Casey Carmichael. Grand Rapids: Reformation Heritage, 2014.

Cunha, Stephen M. *The Emperor Has No Clothes: Dr. Richard B. Gaffin Jr.'s Doctrine of Justification.* Unicoi, TN: Trinity Foundation, 2008.

Dennison, William. Review of VanDrunen's *Natural Law and the Two Kingdoms. WTJ* 75 (2013) 349–70.

Dennison, James T., et al. "Merit or 'Entitlement' in Reformed Covenant Theology: A Review," *Kerux* 24 3 (2009).

Elam, Andrew M., et al., eds. *Merit and Moses: A Critique of the Klinean Doctrine of Republication.* Eugene, OR: Wipf & Stock, 2014.

Estelle, Bryan D., et al., eds. *The Law Is Not of Faith: Essays on Works and Grace in the Mosaic Covenant.* Phillipsburg, NJ: P&R, 2009.

Bibliography

Ferry, Brenton C. "Cross-Examining Moses' Defense: An Answer To Ramsey's Critique Of Kline And Karlberg." *WTJ* 67 (2005) 163–68.

———. "Works in the Mosaic Covenant: A Reformed Taxonomy." ThM thesis, Westminster Theological Seminary, 2009.

Fesko, John V. *The Theology of the Westminster Standards*. Wheaton, IL: Crossway, 2014.

Frame, John M. *Systematic Theology: An Introduction to Christian Belief*. Phillipsburg: P&R, 2013.

Franke, John R. *The Character of Theology: A Postconservative Evangelical Approach*. Grand Rapids: Baker Academic, 2005.

Gaffin, Richard B., Jr. *By Faith, Not by Sight: Paul and the Order of Salvation*. Phillipsburg: P&R, 2014.

———. "For Us and for Our Salvation." In *New Horizons*, 38 4 (2017) 3–5.

Godfrey, W. Robert and D. G. Hart. *Westminster Seminary California: A New Old School*. Escondido: Westminster Seminary California, 2012.

Golding, Peter. *Covenant Theology: The Key of Theology in Reformed Thought and Tradition*. Ross-shire: Mentor, 2004.

Gruenler, Royce G. *The Trinity in the Gospel of John: A Thematic Commentary on the Fourth Gospel*. Grand Rapids, Baker, 1986.

Hagopian, David. G., ed. *The Genesis Debate: Three Views on the Days of Creation*. Mission Viejo, CA: Crux, 2001.

Helyer, Larry R. *The Witness of Jesus, Paul and John: An Exploration in Biblical Theology*. Westmont, IL: InterVarsity, 2008.

Hooykaas, R. *Religion and the Rise of Modern Science*. Grand Rapids: Eerdmans, 1972.

Hughes, John J., ed. *Speaking the Truth in Love: The Theology of John M. Frame*. Phillipsburg: P&R, 2009.

Irons, Lee. "Redefining Merit: An Examination of Medieval Presuppositions in Covenant Theology." In *Creator, Redeemer, Consummator: A Festschrift for Meredith G. Kline*. Howard Griffith and John R. Muether, eds. Reformed Theological Seminary, 2000.

Johnson, Gary L. W. and Guy P. Waters, eds. *By Faith Alone: Answering the Challenges to the Doctrine of Justification*. Wheaton, IL: Crossway, 2006.

Jones, Mark. "In What Sense?" Review of *The Law Is Not of Faith*, Ordained Servant 10 (2010) 115–19.

Jeon, Jeong Koo. *Calvin and the Federal Vision*. Eugene, OR: Wipf and Stock, 2009.

———. *Covenant Theology: John Murray's and Meredith G. Kline's Response to the Historical Development of Federal Theology in Reformed Thought*. Lanham, MD: University Press of America, 2004.

———. *Covenant Theology and Justification by Faith: The Shepherd Controversy and Its Impacts*. Eugene, OR: Wipf and Stock, 2006.

Karlberg, Mark W. *Covenant Theology in Reformed Perspective: Collected Essays and Book Reviews in Historical, Biblical, and Systematic Theology*. Eugene, OR: Wipf and Stock, 2000.

———. *Engaging Westminster Calvinism: The Composition of Redemption's Song*. Eugene, OR: Wipf and Stock, 2013.

———. *Federalism and the Westminster Tradition: Reformed Orthodoxy at the Crossroads*. Eugene, OR: Wipf and Stock, 2006.

———. "Fighting the Good Fight: A Bout with John Frame." In *Gospel Grace: The Modern-day Controversy*. Eugene, OR: Wipf and Stock, 2003.

———. *Gospel Grace: The Modern-day Controversy*. Eugene, OR: Wipf and Stock, 2003.

———. "John Frame and the Recasting of Van Tilian Apologetics: A Review Article." In *Mid-America Journal of Theology* 9 (1993) 279–96.

———. *John Piper on the Christian Life: An Examination of His Controversial View of 'Faith Alone'.* In Future Grace. Great Bromley: Christian Research Network, 1999.

———. "Law in Pauline Eschatology: The Historical Qualification of Justification by Faith." ThM thesis. Westminster Theological Seminary, 1977.

———. "Master of Deception and Intrigue: Yet Another Glimpse into the Work and Psyche of Westminster Seminary." In *The Trinity Review.* Special issue, May 2014.

———. "On the Theological Correlation of Divine and Human Language: A Review Article." In *Journal of the Evangelical Theological Society* 32 (1989) 99–105.

———. "Recovering the Mosaic Covenant as Law and Gospel: J. Mark Beach, John H. Sailhamer, and Jason C. Meyer as Representative Expositors." *EvQ* 83 3 (2011) 233–50.

———. *The Changing of the Guard: Westminster Theological Seminary in Philadelphia.* Unicoi, TN: The Trinity Foundation, 2001.

———. "The Significance of Israel in Biblical Typology." *JETS* 31 (1988) 257–69; reprinted in *Covenant Theology in Reformed Perspective.*

———. "The Mosaic Covenant and the Concept of Works in Reformed Hermeneutics: A Historical-critical Analysis with Special Attention to Early Covenant Eschatology." ThD dissertation, Westminster Theological Seminary, 1980.

———. "Troubler of Israel: Report on Republication by the Orthodox Presbyterian Church Assessing the Teaching of Professor Meredith G. Kline." In *The Trinity Review.* Special issue, October 2014.

Kim, Mark. "Michael Horton's Covenant Theology as a Defense of Reformation Theology in the Context of Current Discussions." ThD dissertation, Toronto School of Theology, 2013.

Kline, Meredith G. *God, Heaven and Har Magedon: A Covenant Tale of Cosmos and Telos.* Eugene, OR: Wipf and Stock, 2006.

———. *Images of the Spirit.* Grand Rapids: Baker, 1980.

———. *Glory in our Midst: A Biblical-theological Reading of Zechariah's Night Visions.* Eugene, OR: Wipf and Stock, 2001.

———. *Kingdom Prologue: Genesis Foundations for a Covenantal Worldview.* Eugene, OR: Wipf and Stock, 2006.

———. *The Structure of Biblical Authority.* Grand Rapids: Eerdmans, 1972.

———. "Symbols, Structures, and Scripture." Review of *Christ and Architecture.* D.J. Bruggink and C.H. Droppers. In the *Presbyterian Guardian,* 35 (1966) 74–75.

———. *Treaty of the Great King: The Covenant Structure of Deuteronomy; Studies and Commentary.* Grand Rapids: Eerdmans, 1963.

Lee, Brian. "Reconciling the Two Covenants in the Old Testament." Review of *The Law Is Not of Faith, Ordained Servant* 10 (2010) 120–26.

———. "Why I Hold to Republication." In *Christian Renewal* (2013) 41–43.

Letham, Robert. "'Not a Covenant of Works in Disguise' (Herman Bavinck): The Place of the Mosaic Covenant in Redemptive History." *MAJT* 24 (2013) 143–77.

Lillback, Peter A., ed. *Seeing Christ in All of Scripture: Hermeneutics at Westminster Theological Seminary.* Philadelphia: Westminster Seminary, 2016.

Lillback, Peter A. and Richard B. Gaffin, Jr., eds. *Thy Word is Still Truth: Essential Writings on the Doctrine of Scripture from the Reformation to Today.* Phillipsburg: P&R, 2013.

Machen, J. Gresham. *What is Faith?* Carlisle: The Banner of Truth Trust, 1991.

Bibliography

McGraw, Ryan M. *Christ's Glory, Your Good: Salvation Planned, Promised, Accomplished, and Applied.* Grand Rapids, MI: Reformation Heritage, 2013.

McManigal, Daniel W. *Encountering Christ in the Covenants: An Introduction to Covenant Theology.* West Linn, OR: Monergism, 2013.

Murray, John. *Redemption Accomplished and Applied.* Grand Rapids: Eerdmans, 1955.

Piper, John, Justin Taylor, and Paul Kjoss Helseth, eds. *Beyond the Bounds: Open Theism and the Undermining of Biblical Christianity.* Wheaton, IL: Crossway, 2003.

Rainbow, Paul A. *The Way of Salvation: The Role of Christian Obedience in Justification.* Bletchley, UK: Paternoster, 2005.

Ramsey, D. Patrick. "In Defense of Moses: A Confessional Critique of Kline and Karlberg." *WTJ* 66 (2004) 373–400.

Robbins, John W. *A Companion to the Current Justification Controversy.* Unicoi, TN: The Trinity Foundation, 2003.

Robertson, O. Palmer. *Christ of the Covenants.* Phillipsburg: P&R, 1980.

———. *The Currrent Justification Controversy.* Unicoi, TN: The Trinity Foundation, 2003.

Shepherd, Norman. *The Call of Grace: How the Covenant Illuminates Salvation and Evangelism.* Phillipsburg: P&R, 2000.

Sirota, Victoria. *Preaching to the Choir: Claiming the Role of Sacred Musician.* New York: Church, 2006.

Smith, Ralph. *Eternal Covenant: How the Trinity Reshapes Covenant Theology.* Moscow, Idaho: Canon, 2003.

Sproul, R. C., Sr. *Everyone's a Theologian: An Introduction to Systematic Theology.* Sanford, FL: Reformation Trust, 2014.

Stonehouse, N. B., and Paul Woolley, eds. *The Infallible Word: A Symposium by Members of the Faculty of Westminster Theological Seminary.* Philadelphia: P&R, 1946.

Troxel, A. Craig, et al. "Report of the Committee to Study Republication." Available on the Orthodox Presbyterian Church website: https://www.opc.org/GA/republication.html.

VanDrunen, David. *Divine Covenants and Moral Order: A Biblical Theology of Natural Law.* Emory University Studies in Law and Religion, ed. John Witte, Jr. Grand Rapids: Eerdmans, 2014.

VanDrunen, David. "Israel's Recapitulation of Adam's Probation under the Law of Moses." *WTJ* 73 (2011) 303–24.

Van Drunen, David M., et al. *Justification: Report of the Committee to Study the Doctrine of Justification: Commended for Study by the Seventy-third General Assembly of the Orthodox Presbyterian Church.* Willow Grove, PA: The Committee on Christian Education, 2007.

VanDrunen, David, ed. *The Pattern of Sound Doctrine: Systematic Theology at the Westminster Seminaries.* Phillipsburg: P&R, 2004.

Venema, Cornelis P. *Christ and Covenant Theology.* Phillipsburg: P&R, 2017.

———. "The Mosaic Covenant: A 'Republication' of the Covenant of Works? A Review Article: *The Law is Not of Faith: Essays on Works and Grace in the Mosaic Covenant.*" *MAJT* 21 (2010) 35–101.

———. "*Sic et Non.* Views in Review: II. Westminster Seminary California Distinctives? The Republication of the Covenant of Works." *Confessional Presbyterian* 9 (2013) 157–87.

———. "The Mosaic Covenant: A 'Republication' of the Covenant of Works? A Review Article: *The Law Is Not of Faith: Essays on Works and Grace in the Mosaic Covenant*." In *Mid-America Journal of Theology* 21 (2010) 35–102.

———. "The Republication of the Covenant of Works." In *Confessional Presbyterian* 8 (2012) 197–227.

Vos, Geerhardus. *Biblical Theology: Old and New Testaments*. Grand Rapids: Eerdmans, 1954.

Ward, Rowland S. *God and Adam: Reformed Theology and the Creation Covenant*. Wantrina, Australia: New Melbourne, 2003.

Weber, Otto. *Foundations of Dogmatics*. Volume One. Grand Rapids: Eerdmans, 1981.

Wells, David F. *God in the Whirlwind: How the Holy-love of God Reorients Our World*. Wheaton, IL: Crossway, 2014.

———. *No Place for Truth: Or Whatever Happened to Evangelical Theology?* Grand Rapids: Eerdmans, 1993.

Willour, Geoffrey. Review of Ryan M. McGraw's *Christ's Glory, Your Good: Salvation Planned, Promised, Accomplished, and Applied*. In *New Horizons* (2013) 21–22.

Woolsey, Andrew. *Unity and Continuity in Covenantal Thought*. Grand Rapids, MI: Reformation Heritage, 2012.

Name Index

Adams, Jay, 77n19
Augustine, 7

Bahsen, Greg L., 108
Barker, William S. II, 106n23
Barth, Karl, 71, 83, 93, 121n17
Bavinck, Herman, 19, 124n24
Beach, J. Mark, 84n30, 97n15
Beale, Gregory K., 75
Beisner, E. Calvin, 92n10
Bergquist, Randall A., 93n10
Berkhof, Hendrikus, 41, 42n6, 45n9, 50n15
Berkhof, Louis, 19, 43n7
Berkouwer, G. C., 121
Binning, Hugh, 83–85
Boice, James M., 80n21
Braun, Johannus, 93
Brown, Mark, 84n30
Brown, Michael, 92n10, 93n7
Bultmann, Rudolf, 16

Calvin, John, 132
Clark, Scott, 113n1
Clowney, Edmund P., 71–72, 82n27, 106n23
Cocceius, Johannus, 84n30
Collenridge, Mark A., 93n10, 105n21
Conn, Harvie, 72, 108n25, 111
Cunha, Stephen M., 80n22, 107n23

Davis. D. Clair, 78, 104n20, 125
DeGraaf, S. G., 121
Dennison, James T., 92n10, 104n19, 108n24
Dennison, William, 76n16
Dillard, Raymond B., 73, 108n25, 125
Duncan, Ligon, 124n24

Edgar, William, 73
Elam, Andrew M., 93n10
Enns, Peter, 73, 77–78, 81, 108n25, 125
Estelle, Bryan D., 92n9, 92n10, 106

Ferguson, Sinclair B., 73, 78, 80n21, 116n5, 125
Ferry, Brenton Clark, 92n10, 97n15, 108n24
Fesko, John V., 93n10, 108n24
Frame, John M., x, 29, 44n8, 73–77, 106n23, 107–8, 111, 119n12
Franke, John, 29–32, 44n8

Gaffin, Richard B., Jr., 71, 73, 76, 77n17, 78n20, 80, 82, 85, 87n2, 90n4, 103, 104n19, 106–8, 111, 114–15, 118, 119n12, 125–26
Garner, David, 73, 80, 125
Godfrey, W. Robert, 85, 106n23, 125
Golding, Peter, 116n6
Goligher, Liam, 80n21

Name Index

Gordon, T. David, 90n5
Green, Douglas, 108n25
Grenz, Stanley, 30
Gruenler, Royce, 40n2

Handel, George Frederick, 48
Hart, Darryl G., 91n7, 106n23, 126n27
Hauerwas, Stanley, 31
Helseth, Paul Kjoss, 55n4
Helyer, Larry R., 83n29
Hooykass, R., 56n6
Horton, Michael S., 84n30, 104n19

Inks, David, 93n10
Irons, Charles Lee, 91n7, 92n10, 107n23

Jeon, Jeong Koo, 83n29, 125
Jones, Mark, 107n23, 118
Juodaitis, Tom, 105n20

Keele, Zach, 92n10
Kim, Mark, 84n30
Kingsbury, Matthew W., 92
Kline, Meredith G., ix, 45n9, 46n10, 48n13, 52n2, 60n8, 62n11, 64–66, 71, 86, 87–112, 114, 119–25, 133n3
Knox, John Edward, 91, 92n8
Kuschke, Arthur, 107n23

Lee, Brian, 92n10, 93n10
Letham, Robert, 124n24
Lillback, Peter A., 72–73, 80, 108n25, 109n25, 125
Longman, Tremper III, 108n25
Luther, Martin, 8, 12, 19, 26

MacCartney, Dan, 78, 125
Machen, J. Gresham, 29n1, 75, 108n25, 126n27
MacLean, Donald John, 83–84
Marcion, 6
Martin, Andrew J., 84n30
McGraw, Ryan M., 78n20
McManigal, Daniel W., 84n30
McNeill, Brett A., 93n10, 105n21
Meyer, Jason C., 85n30

Mickens, Robert, 86n33
Muller, Richard A., 125n24
Murray, John, 50n15, 83, 84n30, 88, 90, 91n7, 93n11, 103n19, 108, 117–18, 119n12, 121, 123–24, 125n24, 126

Oliphant, Scott, 73

Packer, J. I., 74n12
Pelagius, 12
Piper, John, 55n4, 80
Poythress, Vern, 108n25

Rainbow, Paul A., 77n17
Ramsey, D. Patrick, 97n15
Reynolds, Gregory, 104n20
Robbins, John, 106n22
Robertson, O. Palmer, 99, 106n22, 121n17
Rookmaaker, Hans, 133n4
Rutherford, Samuel, 84
Ryken, Philip G., 80n21

Sailhamer, John H., 85n30
Sanborn, Scott F., 104n19, 108n24
Shepherd, Norman, x, 39n2, 41n4, 71–78, 82–85, 87n2, 88–89, 91n6, 102n18, 103–26
Shishko, William, 107n23
Silva, Moisés, 73, 125
Sirota, Victoria, 134n4
Smith, Ralph, 39n2
Sproul, R. C., Sr., 81–82, 106n23
Spykman, Gordon, 29
Strimple, Robert, 106n23, 107
Swinburnson, Benjamin W., 92n9, 104n19, 108n24

Taylor, Justin, 55n4
Tertullian, 7–8
Tipton, Lane, 92n9, 125
Torrance, Thomas F., 83
Troxel, Craig, 92n9
Trueman, Carl, 73, 125
Trumper, Timothy, 125
Turretin, Francis, 84n30

Name Index

Van Dixhoorn, Chad, 92n9
VanDrunen, David M., 76n16, 90n4, 93n10, 122n20
Van Kooten, Robert C., 93n10
Van Til, Cornelius, ix, x, 19, 24, 39n1, 40n3, 42n6, 42n13, 64–66
Van Til, Salomon, 93
Venema, Cornelis P., 90n5, 92n10, 97n15, 107n23, 114n3, 117–24
Vos, Geerhardus, 19, 61n10, 62, 103n19, 111, 113

Ward, Roland, 92n10
Weber, Otto, 19, 20n7
Wells, David F., 77n18
Willour, Geoffrey, 78n20
White, R. Fowler, 92n10
Woolsey, Andrew, 84n30, 124n24

Young, Edward J., 48n13

www.ingramcontent.com/pod-product-compliance
Lightning Source LLC
Chambersburg PA
CBHW060824190426
43197CB00038B/2258